The Literary Heritage

THE LITERARY HERITAGE

A New Anthology of Prose and Short Story

HARI MOHAN PRASAD

IVAN KHRISTO MASIH

CHAKRADHAR PRASAD SINGH

MOTILAL BANARSIDASS

Delhi • Mumbai • Chennai • Kolkata

Bengaluru • Varanasi • Patna

5th Reprint: Delhi, 2017
First Edition: 2004

ISBN: 978-81-208-2921-3

MOTILAL BANARSIDASS
41 U.A., Bungalow Road, Jawahar Nagar, Delhi 110 007
8 Mahalaxmi Chamber, 22 Bhulabhai Desai Road, Mumbai 400 026
203 Royapettah High Road, Mylapore, Chennai 600 004
236, 9th Main III Block, Jayanagar, Bengaluru 560 011
8 Camac Street, Kolkata 700 017
Ashok Rajpath, Patna 800 004
Chowk, Varanasi 221 001

Printed in India

by RP Jain at NAB Printing Unit,
A-44, Naraina Industrial Area, Phase I, New Delhi–110028
and published by JP Jain for Motilal Banarsidass
41 U.A. Bungalow Road, Jawahar Nagar, Delhi-110007

Preface

Most often students of English make a second-level choice for reading prose pieces and stories. They are seized with the idea that poetry, drama and novel are cornerstones of creative writing; the rest is dross or marginal. This notion needs to be corrected. Stories and prose writings are also significant units of literary activities. In a short space demanding less time, they offer prisms of reality, treasures of ideas and streams of entertainment.

This anthology is not to be claimed as an anthology with a difference, but it definitely serves a reference. It has been prepared with the objective to offer undergraduate students the little wonders of writings both by the English and Indians. They wrote English with competence and sometimes even with excellence. They offer variety of style and multiplicity of themes; they instruct or entertain, elevate or ennoble. We hope our students will not only enjoy reading them; they will also benefit themselves in more than one way.

—H. M. Prasad

—I. K. Masih

—C. P. Singh

CONTENTS

SECTION 'A'

SECTION 'B'

THE CHALLENGE OF OUR TIME

E. M. FORSTER

Temperamentally, I am an individualist. Professionally I am a writer, and my books emphasize the importance of personal relationships and the private life, for I believe in them. What can a man with such an equipment, and with no technical knowledge, say about the challenge of our time ? Like everyone else, I can see that our world is in a terrible mess, and having been to India last winter I know that starvation and frustration can reach proportions unknown to these islands. Wherever I look. I can see, in the striking phrase of Robert Bridges, 'the almighty cosmic Will fidgetting in a trap'. But who set the trap, and how was it sprung ? If I knew, I might be able to unfasten it. I do not know. How can I answer a challenge which I cannot interpret ? It is like shouting defiance at a big black cloud. Some of the other speakers share my diffidence here, I think. Professor Bernal does not. He perceives very precisely what the challenge of our time is and what is the answer to it. Professor Bernal's perceptions are probably stronger than mine. They are certainly more selective, and many things which interest or upset me do not enter his mind at all—or enter it in the form of cards to be filed for future use.

I belong to the fag-end of Victorian liberalism, and can look back to an age whose challenges were moderate in their tone, and the cloud on whose horizon was no higher than a man's hand. I many ways it was an admirable age. It practised benevolence and philanthropy, was humane and intellectually curious, upheld free speech, had little colour prejudice, believed that individuals are and should be different, and entertained a sincere faith in the progress of society. The world was to become better and better, chiefly through the spread of parliamentary institutions. The education I received in those far-off and fantastic days made me soft and I am very glad it did, for I have seen plenty of hardness since, and I know it does not even pay. Think of the end of Mussolini—the hard man, hanging upside-down like a turkey, with his dead mistress swinging beside him.

But though the education was humane it was imperfect, in as much as we none of us realized our economic position. In came the nice fact dividends, up rose the lofty thoughts, and we did not realise that all the time we were exploiting the poor of our own country and the backward races abroad, and getting bigger profits from our investments than we should. We refused to face this unpalatable truth. I remember being told as a small boy. 'Dear, don't talk about money, it's ugly'—a good example that of Victorian defence mechanism.

All that has changed in the present century. The dividends have shrunk to decent proportions and have in some cases disappeared. The poor have kicked. The backward races are kicking—and more power to their boots. Which means that life has become less comfortable for the Victorian liberal, and that our outlook, which seems to me admirable, has lost the basis of golden sovereigns upon which it originally rose, and now hangs over the abyss. I indulge in these reminiscences because they lead to the point I want to make.

If we are to answer the challenge of our time successfully, we must manage to combine the new economy and the old morality. The doctrine of *laissez-faire* will not work in the material world. It has led to the black market and the capitalist jungle. We must have planning and ration books and controls, or millions of people will have nowhere to live and nothing to eat. On the other hand, the doctrine of *laissez-faire* is the only one that seems to work in the world of the spirit; if you plan and control men's minds you stunt them, you get the censorship, the secret police, the road to serfdom, the community of slaves. Our economic planners sometimes laugh at us when we are afraid of totalitarian tyranny resulting from their efforts—or rather they sneer at us, for there is some deep connection between planning and sneering which psychologists should explore. But the danger they brush aside is a real one. They assure us that the new economy will evolve an appropriate morality, and that when all people are properly fed and housed, they will have an outlook which will be right, because they are the people. I cannot swallow that. I have no mystic faith in the people. I have in the individual. He seems to me a divine achievement and I mistrust any view which belittles him. If anyone calls you a wretched little individual—and I've been called that—don't you take it lying down. You are important because everyone else is an individual too—including the person who criticizes you. In asserting your personality you are playing for your side.

That then is the slogan with which I would answer, or partially answer, The Challenge of Our Time. We want the new economy with the old morality. We want planning for the body and not for the spirit. But the difficulty is this : where does the body stop and the spirit start ? In the Middle Ages a hard and fast line was drawn between them, and according to the mediaeval theory of the Holy Roman Empire men rendered their bodies to Caesar and their souls to God. But the theory did not work. The Emperor, who represented Christ, collided in practice with the Pope, who represented Christ. And we find ourselves in a similar dilemma today. Suppose you are planning the world-distribution of food. You can't do that without planning world population. You can't do that without regulating the number of births and interfering with family life. You must supervise parenthood. You are meddling with the realms of the spirit, of personal relationship, although you may not have intended to do so. And you are brought back again to that inescapable arbiter, your own temperament. When there is a collision of principles would you favour the individual at the expense of the community as I would ? Or would you prefer economic justice for all the expense of personal freedom ?

In a time of upheaval like the present, this collision of principles, this split in one's loyalties, is always occurring. It has just occurred in my own life. I was brought up as a boy in one of the home countries, in a district which I still think the loveliest in England. There is nothing special about it—it is agricultural land, and could not be described in terms of beauty spots. It must always have looked much the same. I have kept in touch with it, going back to it as to an abiding city and still visiting the house which was once my home, for it is occupied by friends. A farm is through the hedge, and when the farmer there was eight years old and I was nine, we used to jump up and down on his grandfather's straw ricks and spoil them. Today he is a grandfather himself, so that I have the sense of five generations continuing in one place. Life went on there as usual until this spring. Then someone who was applying for a permit to lay a water pipe was casually informed that it would not be granted since the whole area had been commandeered. Commandeered for what ? Had not the war ended ? Appropriate officials of the Ministry of Town and Country Planning now arrived from London and announced that a satellite town for 60,000 people is to be built. The people now living and working there are dosmed : it is death in life for them and they move in a nightmare. The best agricultural land has been taken, they assert; the poor land down by the railway has been left; compensation is inadequate. Anyhow, the satellite town has finished them off as completely as it will obliterate the ancient and delicate scenery. Meteorite town would be a better name. It has fallen out of a blue sky.

'Well', says the voice of planning and progress, 'Why this sentimentality? People must have houses'. They must, and I think a working-class friends in north London who have to bring up four children in two rooms, and many are even worse off than that. But I cannot equate the problem. It is a collision of loyalties. I cannot free myself from the conviction that something irreplaceable has been destroyed, and that a little piece of England has died as surely as if a bomb had hit it. I wonder what compensation there is in the world of the spirit, for the destruction of the life here, the life of tradition.

These are personal reminiscence and I am really supposed to be speaking from the standpoint of the creative artist. But you will gather what a writer, who also cares for men and women and for the countryside, must be feeling in the world today. Uncomfortable, of course. Sometimes miserabie and indignant. But convinced that a planned change must take place if the world is not to disintegrate and hopeful that in the new economy there may be a sphere both for human relationships, and for the despised activity known as art. What cught the writer, the artist, to do when faced by the challenge of our time ? Briefly, he ought to express what he wants and not what he is told to express by the planning authorities. He ought to impose a discipline on himself rather than accept one from outside. And that discipline may be aesthetic, rather than social or moral; he may wish to practise art for art's sake. That phrase has been foolishly used and often raises a giggle. But it is a profound phrase. It indicates that art is a self-contained harmony. Art is valuable not because it is educational (thought it may be), not because it is recreative (thought it may be), not because everyone enjoys it (for everybody does not), not even because it has to do with order, and creates little worlds of its own, possessing internal harmony, in the bosom of this disordered planet, It is needed at once and now. It is needed before it is appreciated and independent of appreciation. The idea that it should not be permitted until it receives communal acclaim and unless it is for all, is perfectly absurd. It is the activity which brought man out of original darkness and differentiates him from the beasts, and we must continue to practise and respect it through the darkness of today.

I am speaking like an intellectual, but the intellectual, to my mind, is more in touch with humanity than is the confident scientist, who patronizes the past, over-simplifies the present, and envisages a future where his leadership will be accepted. Owing to the political needs of the moment, the scientist occupies an abnormal position, which he tends to forget. He is subsidized by the terrified governments who need his aid, pampered and sheltered as long as he is obedient, and prosecuted under Official Secrets Acts when he had been naughty. All this separates him from ordinary men and women and makes him unfit to enter into their feelings. It is high time he came out of his ivory laboratory. We want him to plan for our bodies. We do not want him to plan for our minds, and we cannot accept, so far, his assurance that he will not.

THE CHALLENGE OF OUR TIME

About the Author

E. M. Forster (1879-1970) is an English novelist who belonged to the "Bloomsburys Group". It was a cotorie of writers and intellectuals with a common interest in love, art and truth and revulsion against Victorian inhibitions.

He is a writer with a keen eye for idiosyncracies of temperament and the capacity of people to deceive themselves. Forster is dualistic in approach and tried to bridge gap between different races and nationalities, specially in his famous novel **A Passage to India** he is prophetically emphatic on establishment of human relationships if not now then definitely in future. He had a good insight in Indian life and philosophy and respected Indian values. He also had a spiritual dimension.

This essay by E. M. Forster presents his concern for the world of today hurtling towards a situation in which human values have been neglected. Scientific advancement may be political compulsion but ignoring of moral values of the past is self defeating. He is apparently against materialistic system which supports elitism. He advocates a combination of new economic order with the old morality.

Reference

Abyss — *deep immeasurable space, infinite*

Reminiscences — *the process of recalling the past, a recollection retold.*

Aesthetic — *pertaining to a sense of the beautiful, sensation as opposed to pure intellectuality.*

❑

INDIA AGAIN

E. M. FORSTER

It was a dull, cold Friday morning in October, 1945 when I left England. Two days later, on the Sunday afternoon. I was in India. Below me lay the desert of Rajputana, baked by the sun and blotched with the shadows of clouds. The plane came down for half an hour near the dragon-shaped fort of Jodhpur, then took off again, and it was Delhi. I felt dazed. And we had travelled so fast that we were ahead of schedule, and had no one to meet us. Suddenly very slow, instead of very quick, we jogged in a tonga through the Delhi bazaars, our luggage in front; our legs hanging down behind, the dust rising, the sun setting, the smoke drifting out of the little shops. It became dark and the sky was covered with stars. Were we lost ? No. An unknown host, an Indian, received us, and next day I stood on the high platform of the Great Mosque, one of the noblest buildings in India and the world. Profound thankfulness filled me. The sky was now intensely blue, the kites circled round and round the pearlgrey domes and the red frontispiece of sand-stone, sounds drifted up from Delhi city, the pavement struck warm through the soles of my socks; I was back in the country I loved, after an absence of twenty-five years.

I was bound for a conference of Indian writers. The All India centre of the P.E.N. Club had invited us. The people I was to meet were nearly all Indians, of the professional classes—doctors, lawyers, public servants, professors at the university, businessmen. Many of them were old friends or the sons of old friends. They were what is termed 'intellectuals' and they lived in towns. I did not see much of the countryside nor of the industrial conditions. I met a few Englishmen but not many, and have often looked round a crowded room and observed that I was the only westerner in it. Such are my credentials, or if you prefer, such are my limitations.

The big change I noticed was the increased interest in politics. You cannot understand the modern Indians unless you realize that politics occupy them passionately and constantly, that artistic problems, and even social problems—yes and even economic problems—are subsidiary. Their attitude is 'first we must find the correct political solution, and then we can deal with other matters.' I think the attitude is unsound and used to say so; still, there it is, and they hold it much more vehemently than they did a quarter of a century ago. When I spoke about the necessity of form in literature and the importance of the individual vision, their attention wandered although they listened politely. Literature, in their view. should expound or inspire a political creed.

Externally the place has not changed. It looks much as it did from the train. Outside the catriage windows (the rather dirty windows) it unrolls as before—monotonous, enigmatic, and at moments sinister, And in some long motor drives which I took through the Deccan there were the same combinations of hill, rock, bushes, ruins, dusty people and occasional yellow flowers which I encountered when I walked on the soil in my youth. There is still poverty, and since I am older today and more thoughtful, it is the poverty, the malnutrition, which persists like a ground-swell beneath the pleasant froth of my immediate experience, I do not know what political solution is correct. But I do know that people ought not to be so poor and to look so ill, and that rats ought not to run about them as I saw them doing in a labour camp at Bombay. Industrialism has increased, though it does not dominate the landscape yet as it does in the west. You can see the chimneys of the cotton mills at Ahmedabad, but you can see its mosques too. You can see little factories near Calcutta, but they are tucked away amongst bananas and palms, and the one I have in mind has a an enormous tree overhanging it in whose branches a witch is said to sit, and from whose branches huge fruit occasionally fall and hit the corrugated iron roofs with a bang so that the factory hands jump. No—externally India has not changed." And this changelessness in her is called by some observers 'the real India'. I don't myself like the phrase 'the real India.' I suspect it. It always makes me prick up my ears. But you can use it if you want to, either for the changes in her or for the unchanged. 'Real' is at the service of all schools of thoughts.

It is when you leave the country, or the streets of the town, and go into the private houses, that you begin to notice a second great alteration, second only to politics—namely, the lifting of purdah, the increasing emancipation of women. It struck me particularly in cities which are largely Moslem, such as Lahore and Hyderabad, where women once kept rigidly behind the veil. I have been in my life three times to Hyderabad, some of my happiest Indian days were spent there, so I have been able to trace this change. My first visit was in 1912 and then I saw scarcely any Indian women. My second visit was in 1921, when I was admitted into some family circles and saw a good deal of what may be called 'semipurdah'—ladies coming out into company, but not coming avowedly, and retiring at any moment behind the veil if they felt disposed to do so. Today, purdha has broken down at Hyderabad, except amongst the most conservative, and at the receptions to which I went the women sometimes outnumbered the men. Since they kept to their lovely Indian saris the effect was exquisite, it was a delight to look round at so much gracefulness and graciousness, at so many and such well chosen colours. I don't know how far into society this lifting of the veil has extended. But I imagine that sooner or later the change will extend to the villages and transform the Indian social fabric from top to bottom. Our world does not go back, though whether it progresses God alone knows and in India, as in the west women will shortly have the same opportunities as men for good and for evil.

The reception I have been mentioning usually took the form of buffet dinners they are an innovation since my time. Long tables are loaded with Indian food, and sometimes one table is labelled 'vegetarian' and the other 'non-vegetarian'. You help yourself or are helped. I take away pleasant memories of these buffet dinners, memories of Indians moving elegantly through well-filled rooms, with well-filled plates in their hands, and miraculously conveying food to their mouths in the folds of a chappati. There is rationing, but its workings are mysterious and I did not grasp them or suffer from them. For the well-to-do, life is much easier in India than in England. The shops are full of tinned delicacies for those who can afford them—butter, cheese, even plum puddings. For the poor, life is much harder there than here.

The Indians I met mostly talked English. Some of them spoke very well, and one or two of them write in our language with great distinction.

Why talk English at all ? This question was hotly debated at the P.E.N. conference of All-India Writers. Writers from central or upper India were in favour of Urdu or Hindi as a common language for the whole peninsula. Writers from Bengal, favoured Bengali, and it has claims from the literary point of view. Writers from the south, on the other hand, preferred English. The debate, if I may say so, continues, and into it, as into everything, come politics. I mention it to indicate the trend of events, the change in emphasis. Meanwhile, in this uneasy interregnum English does get talked and gets interlarded in the oddest way with the Indian vernacular. I was travelling one day to Baroda in a crowded second class carriage. Indians, my luggage, their luggage, myself and a number of loose oranges were piled up together in confusion, and the Indians were arguing. Their language was Gujrati, but they used so many English words that I followed what they were saying. They were arguing about religion and free thought. I intervened and was welcomed into the conversation, which was now carried on entirely in English out of courtesy to me. I did not follow it the better for that, but they peeled me an orange and we parted friends. Indeed, it is difficult to conclude an Indian railway journey on any other note. Their response to ordinary civility is immediate. I don't think they are particularly friendly in the street—if you ask them the way they are suspicious. But squashed in a railway carriage they seem to expand. And my reason for wanting English to be the common language for India is a purely selfish reason : I like these chance encounters, I value far more the relationship of years, and if Indians had not spoken English my own life would have been infinitely poorer.

My visit ended all too soon. On a Friday afternoon in December—it was again a Friday. I was walking about in the sunshine of Karachi. And on the Sunday evening I was in London. Our train was icy cold, it arrived at Waterloo two hours late, midnight, thick fog, refreshment-rooms closed, waiting-rooms closed, local trains gone, no taxi could leave the station. It was not much of a return, it was not like the arrival in Delhi.

INDIA AGAIN

About the Author

Edward Morgan Forster (1879-1970) essayist, novelist, critic is considered perhaps the greatest English novelist of the present century. He has a special appeal for Indians because of his sympathetic understanding of India and Indian conditions. **A Passage to India**, his masterpiece describes intimate relationship between Indians and Britishers.

Forster visited India thrice. His last visit to India was made in 1945. He had come to attend the P.E.N. conference at Jaipur. On his return from India, he gave two broadcast talks on B.B.C. which marked his impression of India and Indians. The present piece is an abridgement of one of his talks, and is a model of elegant conversational prose of to-day.

Forster appears to be extremely fair and impartial in his views and very few of us will have any complain against what he says about the overwhelming importance of politics in present day life, the lifting of purdah system among muslim women, the emancipation of women as a class, the poverty and malnutrition of the people and above all the decline in the quality of English spoken by the Indians to-day.

References

Blotched	— spotted
Credentials	— letters of introduction and testimonials.
Subsidiary	— serving as a help or support.
Creed	— system of belief.
Groundswell	— heavy, slow moving waves.
Sinister	— suggesting evil.
Delicacies	— different kinds of tasty food.
Interregnum	— interval
Interlarded	— mixed with

❑

ALL ABOUT A DOG

A.G. GARDINER

It is a bitterly cold night, and even at the far end of the bus the east wind that raved along the street cut like a knife. The bus stopped, and two women and a man got in together and filled the vacant places. The younger woman was dressed in sealskin and carried one of those little Pekinese dogs that women in sealskin like to carry in their laps. The conductor came in and took the fares. Then his eye rested with cold malice on the beady-eyed toy dog. I saw trouble brewing. This was the opportunity for which he had been waiting and he intended to make the most of it. I had marked him as the type of what Mr. Wells had called the Resentful Employee, the man with a general vague grievance against everything and particular grievances against passengers who came and sat in his bus while he shivered at the door.

"You must take that dog out," he said with sour venom.

"I shall certainaly do nothing of the kind. You can take my name and address," said the woman, who had evidently expected the challenge and knew the reply.

"You must take that dog out—that's my orders."

"I won't go on the top in such weather. It would kill me," said the woman.

"Certainly not," said her lady companion. "You've got a cough as it is."

"It's nonsense", said her male companion.

The conductor pulled the bell and the bus stopped. "This bus doesn't go on until that dog is brought out." And he stepped on to the pavement and waited. It was his moment of triumph. He had the law on his side and a whole busful of angry people under the harrow. His embittered soul was having a real holiday.

The storm inside rose high, "Shameful." "He's no better than a German."

"Why isn't he in the army ?" "Call the police." "Let's all report him." "Let's make him give us our fares back." "Yes, that's it, let's make him give us our fares back." For everybody was on the side of the lady and the dog.

That little animal sat blinking at the dim lights in happy unconsciousness of the rumpus of which he was the cause.

The conductor came to the door. "What's your number ?" said one, taking out a pocketbook with a gesture of terrible things. "There's my number," said the conductor imperturbably. "Give us our fares back. You've engaged to carry us—you can't leave us here all night." "No fares back," said the conductor.

Two or three passengers got out and disappeared into the night. The conductor took another turn on the pavement then went and had a talk with the driver. Another bus, the last, on the road, sailed by, indifferent to the shouts of the passengers to stop. "They stick by each other—the villains," was the comment.

Someone pulled the bell violently. That brought the driver round to the door. "Who's conductor of this bus ?" he said, and paused for a reply. None coming, he returned to his seat and resumed beating his arms across his chest. There was no hope in that quarter. A policeman strolled up and looked in at the door. An avalanche of indignant protests and appeals burst on him. "Well, he's got his rules, you know," he said genially. "Given your name and address ?" "That's what has been offered, and he won't take it." "Oh," said the policeman, and he went away and took his stand a few yards down the street, where he was joined by two more constables.

And still the little dog blinked at the lights, and the conductor walked to and fro on the pavement, like a captain on the quarter-deck in the hour of victory. A young woman, whose voice had risen high above the gale inside descended on him with an air of threatening and slaughter. He was immovable as cold as the night and hard as the pavement. She passed on in a fury of impotence to the three policemen who stood like a group of statutes up the street watching the drama. Then she came back, imperiously beckoned to her 'young man' who had sat a silent witness of her rage, and vanished. Others followed. The bus was emptying. Even the dashing young fellow who had demanded the number, and who had declared he would see this thing through, if he sat there all night, had taken an opportunity to slip away.

Meanwhile the Pekinese party were passing through every stage of resistance to abject surrender. "I'll go on the to P", said the sealskin lady at last. "You mustn't." "I will. You will have pneumonia." "Let me take, it." This from the man "Certainly not"—she would die with her dog. When she had disappeared up the stairs, the conductor came back, pulled the bell, and the bus went on. He stood sourly triumphant while his conduct was savagely discussed in his face by the remnant of the party.

Then the engine struck work, and the conductor went to the help of the driver. It was along job, and precrisly the lady with the dog stole down the stairs and re-entered the bus when the engine was put right, the conductor came back and pulled the bell. Then his eye fell on the dog, and his hand went on the bell-rope again. The driver looked round. The conductor pointed to the dog, the bus stopped, and the struggle recommenced with all the original features, the conductor walking the pavement, the driver smacking his arms on the box, the little dog blinking at the lights, the sealskin lady declaring that she would not go on the top—and finally going.

"I've got my rules," said the conductor to me when I was the last passenger left behind. He had won his victory but felt that he would like to justify himself to somebody.

"Rules," I said, "are necessary things, but there are rules and rules. Some are hard and fast rules, like the rule of the road, which cannot be broken without danger to life and limb. But some are only rules for your guidance, which you can apply or wink at, as commonsense dictates—like that rule about the dogs. They are not a whip put in your hand to scourge your passengers with, but an authority for an emergency. They are meant to be observed in the spirit, not in the letter—for the comfort and not the discomfort of the passengers. You have kept the rule and broken its spirit. You want to mix your rules with a little goodwill and good temper."

He took it very well, and when I got off the bus he said, "Good night", quite amiably.

ALL ABOUT A DOG

About the Author

A. G. Gardiner (1865-1946) wrote under the pen name of Alpha of the Plough. He was basically a journalist who wrote delightful and entertaining essays on common subjects. He displays a sense of wit, humour and also of irony in his writings. His writings provoke the readers to discuss the subtle reality which is many times missed in the maze of appearance. His language is lucid and his expressions are straight, conversational but they have many times, more than appearance meaning. The implied irony enriches his writings.

In this essay he shows how a man may be right according to the letter of the law but wrong according to the spirit of the law. If we look around many of our problems arise from our lack of the desire to go by the spirit of the law. The spirit of the law is also positive and its aim is upright justice to all without any discrimination.

References

Bitterly — unpleasant

East wind — the wind most feared in England.

Cut like a knife — hurt severly

Sealskin — a fur coat under the skin of seals.

Pekinese dogs — small beautiful dogs.

Beady-eyed — small eyes

Toy dog — small pet dog

Mr. Wells — H. G. Wells, English novlist.

Storm rose high — anger increased

Rumpus — a noisy quarrel

Avalanche — great mass of snow and ice rushing down a mountain side. Here it suggests the angry words of the passengers

Hard and fast — rigid

In the spirit — for the real purpose.

The letter — the exact wording

❑

A WORK OF ART

ANTON P. CHEKHOV

Holding under his arm an object wrapped in a newspaper, Sasha. Smirnov, the only son of his mother, walked nervously into the office of Doctor Keshelkov.

'Well my dear boy', 'exclaimed the doctor warmly, 'how do you feel today ? What's the good news ?'

Sasha began to blink with his eyes, put his hand over his heart, and stammered nervously.

'My mother sends her regards and begs to thank you ... I am my mother's only son, and you have saved my life ... and we both hardly know how to thank you.'

Come, come, my young friend, let us not speak of it, interrupted the doctor, literally melting with pleasure. 'I have only done what anybody else in my place would have done.'

'I am the only son of my mother ... We are poor people and consequently we are not in a position to pay you for your trouble ... and it makes it very embarrassing for us, Doctor, although both of us, mother and I, who am the only son of my mother, beg of you to accept from us as token of our gratitude, this object which ... is an object of rare worth, a wonderful masterpiece in antique bronze."

The doctor made a grimace.

'Why, my dear friend,' he said, 'it is entirely unnecessary. I don't need this in the least.'

'Oh, no, no', stammered Sasha. 'I beg you please accept it !'

He began to unwrap the bundle, continuing his entreaties in the meantime.

'If you do not accept this, you will offend both my mother and myself ... This is a very rare work of art ... an antique bronze, It is a relic left by my dead father. We have been prizing it as a very dear remembrance ... My father used to buy up bronze antiques, selling them to lovers of old statuary ... And now we continue in the same business, my mother and myself.'

Sasha undid the package and enthusiastically placed it on the table.

It was a low candelabrum of antique bronze, a work of real art representing a group : On a pedestal stood two figures of women clad in the costume of mother Eve and in poses that I have neither the audacity nor the temperament to describe. These figures were smiling coquettishly and in general gave one the impression that, were it not for the fact that they were obliged to support the candle-stick, they would lean down from their pedestal and exhibit a performance which ... my dear reader, I am even ashamed to think of it !

When the doctor espied the present, he slowly scratched his head, cleared his throat and blew his nose.

'Yes, indeed a very pretty piece of work,' he mumbled ... But—how shall I say it—not quite ... I mean ... rather unconventional ... not a bit literary, is it ? ... You know ... the devil knows ....

'Why ?'

'Beelzebub himself could not have conceived anything more ugly. Should I place such a phantasmagoria upon my table I would pollute my entire home !'

'Why, Doctor, what a strange conception you have of art !' cried Sasha in offended tones. 'This is a real masterpiece. Just look at it ! Such is its harmonious beauty that just to contemplate it fills the soul with ecstasy and makes the throat choke down a sob ! When you see such loveliness you forget all earthly things ... just look at it ! What life, what motion, what expression !'

'I quite understand all this, my dear boy,' interrupted the doctor. 'But I am a married man. Little children run in and out of this room and ladies come here continually.'

'Of course', said Sasha, 'if you look at it through the eyes of the rabble, you see this noble masterpiece in an entirely different light. But you certainly are above all that,' Doctor, and especially when your refusal to accept this gift will deeply offend both my mother and myself, who am the only son of my mother .... You have saved my life .... and in return we give you our dearest possession and .... my only regret is that we are unable to give you the mate to this candelabrum.

'Thanks, friend, many thanks .... Remember me to your mother and .... But for God's sake ! You can see for yourself, can't you ? Little children run in and out of this room, and ladies come here continually .... However, leave it here ! There's no arguing with you.'

'Don't say another word !' exclaimed Sasha joyously 'Put the candelabrum right here, next to the vase. By Jove, but it's a pity that I haven't got the mate to give you. But it can't be helped. Well, goodbye, Doctor !"

After the departure of Sasha the doctor looked for a long time at the candelabrum and scratched his head.

'This is beautiful, all right' he thought. 'It would be a pity to throw it a away .... And yet I dare not keep it ... Hm ! ... Now who in the world is there whom I can present or donate it ?'

After long deliberation he hit upon a good friend of his, the lawyer Ukhov, to whom he was indebted for legal services.

'Fine !' chuckled the doctor. 'Being a close friend of his I cannot very well offer him money and so I will give him this piece of indecency instead ... And he's just the man for it .... single, and somewhat of a gay bird, too.'

No sooner thought than done, Dressing him self the doctor look the candelabrum and went to the home of Ukhov.

'Good morning old chap !' he said. 'I have come here to thank you for your trouble .... You will not take money, and I will therefore repay you by presenting you with this exquisite masterpiece ... Now say for yourself, isn't it a dream ?'

As soon as the lawyer caught sight of it he was exhilarated with its beauty.

'What a wonderful work of art !" he laughed uproariously. 'Ye gods, what conceptions artists will get in their heads ! What alluring charm ! Where did you get this little dandy ?'

But now his exhilaration had oozed away and he became frightened. Looking stealthily toward the door, he said—

'But, I can't accept it old chap. You must take it right back.'

'Why ?' asked the doctor in alarm.

'Because ... because ... my mother often visits me, my clients come here ... and besides, I would be disgraced even in the eyes of my servants.'

'Don't say another word !' cried the doctor gesticulating wildly. 'You simply have got a accept it ! It would be rank ingratitude for you to refuse it ! Such a masterpiece ! What motion, what expression ... You will greatly offend me if you don't take it !'

'If only this were daubed over or covered with figleaves .... '

But the doctor refused to listen to him. Gesticulating even more wildly, he ran out of Ukhov's house in the thought that he was rid of the present.

When the doctor was gone the lawyer carefully examined the candelabrum, and then, just as the doctor had done, he began to wonder what in the world he could do with it.

'A very beautiful object', he thought. 'It is a pity to throw it away, and yet it is disgraceful to keep it. I had best present it to someone ... I've got it ! ... this very evening I am going to give it to the comedian Shoshkin. The rascal loves such things, besides, this is his benefit night.

No sooner thought than done, That afternoon the well-packed candelabrum was brought to the comedian Shoshkin.

That whole evening the dressing-room of the comedian Shoshkin was besieged by men who hastened to inspect the present. And during all the time the room re-echoed with hilarious laughter which most closely resembled the neighing of horses.

If any of the actresses approached the door and said 'May I enter ?' The hoarse voice of Shoskin was immediately heard to reply—

'Oh, no, no, my darling you mustn't I am not dressed ?'

After the performance the comedian shrugged his shoulders, gesticulated with his hands and said :

'Now what in the world am I to do with this ? I live in a private apartment ! I am often visited by actresses ! and this isn't a photograph that one could conceal in a drawer !'

'Why don't you sell it ?' suggested the wig-maker 'There is a certain old woman who buys up antique. bronzes ... Her name is Smirnova ... You had better take a run over there; they'll show you the place all right, everybody knows her ...

The comedian followed his advice ...

Two days later Keshelkov, his head supported on his hand, was sitting in his office concocting pills. Suddenly the door was opened and into the office rushed Shasha. He was smiling radiantly and his breast heaved with joy ... In his hands he held something wrapped in a newspaper.

'Doctor !' he cried breathlessly. 'Imagine my joy ! As luck would have it, I've just succeeded in getting the mate to your candelabrum ! Mother is so happy ! I am the only son of my mother ... You have saved my life.'

And Sasha, quivering with thankfulness and rapture, placed a candelabrum before the doctor. The latter opened his mouth as if to say something, but uttered not a word ... His power of speech was gone ...

A WORK OF ART

About the Author

Anton P. Chekhov (1860-1904) is a great dramatist and short story writer of Russia. Famous among his books are **The Seagull, Three Sister** and **The Cherry Orchard.** He gives expression to the frustrated longings of the provincial men and hints at the emptiness and pessimism of life with severe irony. He has the power to twist the conventional humorous situations. He has the psychological insight into the behaviour of his characters. He applies his irony equally to children, animals, young people in distress and elderly. He has been influenced by French Naturalism. He provides his short stories with a rare psychological depth unknown before.

A Work of Art is Chekhov's most popular short story. It is a satire on provincial prudery and meanness. The story in short revolves round a candelabrum, a beautiful work of art in antique bronze. Doctor Koshelkov receives it as a present from an old lady whose son's life he has saved. He is impressed by its artistic beauty but thinks it unconventional to put it on the table of the visiting room because it represented two naked figures of smiling women. He knows that it is beautiful but he dare not keep it on display. He presents it to his lawyer friend, Ukhov, who, in turn presents it to the comedian Shoshkin. On the advice of the wig maker the comedian sells it to an old woman who deals in such artistic pieces of bronze. The surprize of the total situation is that this lady turns out to be the same who had presented it to the doctor. Her son again appears before the doctor to present the candelabrum thinking it to be a mate to the first one presented to him earlier. The situation makes the doctor dumb-founded.

It is an obvious satire on the artificiality and hypocrisy of society. People sometimes become slave to the narrow conventional thinking-making them meanminded. They suffer from a false sense of decency and turn their back on objects of truth and beauty. It is a neatly designed story with a unity of impression. The undercurrent of humour and irony makes it lively reading.

References

Candelabrum — an ornamental candle-holder or lamp stand.

Beelzebub — an evil spirit (from Bible, Paradise lost of Milton)

Unconventional — not acceptable in social norm.

Phatasmagoria — a fantastic series of illusive images.

Embarrasing — a state of being in a fix.

Relic — an old piece of past.

Enthusiastically — with a sense of inner pleasure

Audacity — arrogance

Ecstasy — pleasure

Alluring — attractive

❑

A DEFINITION OF A GENTLEMAN

JOHN HENRY NEWMAN

Hence it is almost a definition of a gentleman to say he is one who never inflicts pain. This description is both refined and, as far as it goes, accurate. He is mainly occupied in merely removing the obstacles which hinder the free and unembarrassed action of those about him; and he concurs with their movements rather than takes the initiative himself. His benefits may be considered as parallel to what are called comforts or conveniences in arrangements of a personal nature; like an easy chair or a good fire, which do their part in dispelling cold and fatigue, though nature provides both means of rest and animal heat without them. The true gentleman in like manner carefully avoids whatever may cause a jar a jolt in the minds of those with whom he is cast; —all clashing of opinion, or collision offelling, allre straint, or suspicion, or gloom, or resentment; his great concern being to make every one at their ease and at home. He has his eyes on all his company; he is tender towards the bashful, gentle towards the distant, and merciful towards the absurd; he can recollect to whom he is speaking; he guards against unseasonable allusions, or topics which may irritate; he is seldom prominent in conversation and never wearisome. He makes light of favours while he does them, and seems to be receiving when he is conferring. He never speaks of him self except when compelled, never defends himself by a mere retort, he has no ears for slander or gossip, is scrupulous in imputing motives to those who interfere with him, and interprets everything for the best. He is never mean of little in his disputes, never takes unfair advantages, never mistakes personalities or sharp saying for arguments, or insinuates evil which he dare not say out. From a long-sighted prudence, he observes the maxim of the ancient sage, that we should ever conduct ourselves towards our enemy as if he were one day to be our friend. He has too much good sense to be affronted at insults, he is too well employed to remember injuries, and too indolent to bear malice. He is patient, forbearing, and resigned, on philosophical principles; he submits to pain, because it is inevitable, to bereavement, because it is irreparable, and to death because it is his destiny. If he engages in controversy of any kind, his disciplined intellect preserves him from the blundering discourtesy of better, though less educated minds; who like blunt weapons, tear and hack instead of cutting clean, who mistake the point in argument, waste their strength on trifles, misconceive their adversary, and leave the question more involved than they find it. He may be right or wrong in his opinion, but he is too clear-headed to be unjust; he is as simple as he is forcible, and as brief as he is decisive. Nowhere shall we find greater condour, consideration, indulgence; he throws himself into the minds of his opponents, he accounts of their mistakes. He knows the weakness of human reason as well as its strength, its province and its limits. If he be an unbeliever, he will be to profound and large-minded to ridicule religion or to act against it; he is to wise to be a dogmatist or fanatic in his infidelity. He respects piety and devotion; he even supports institutions as venerable, beautiful, or useful, to which he does not assent; he honours the ministers of religion, and he is contented to decline its mysteries without assailing or denouncing them. He is a friend of religious toleration, and that, not only because his philosophy has taught him to look on all forms of faith with an impartial eye, but also from the gentleness and effeminacy of feeling, which is the attendant on civilisation.

Not that he may not hold a religion too, in his own way, even when he is not a Christian. In that case his religion is one of imagination and sentiment; it is the embodiment of those ideas of the sublime, majestic and beautiful, without which there can be no large philosophy. Sometimes he acknowledges the being of God, sometimes he invents an unknown principle or quality with the attributes of perfection. And this deduction of his reason, or creation of his fancy, he makes the occasion of such excellent thoughts, and the starting-point of so varied and systematic a teaching, that he even seems like a disciple of Christianity itself. From the very accuracy and steadiness of his logical powers, he is able to see what sentiments are consistent in those who hold any religious doctrine at all, and he appears to others to feel and to hold a whole circle of theological truths which exist in his mind no otherwise than as a number of deductions.

A DEFINITION OF A GENTLEMAN

About the Author

John Henry Newman (1801-1890) was 19th century cardinal and has written profusely on religious and moralistic topics. He was a notable figure of the Oxford movement. An the vicar of St. Mary's, people looked up to him for moral guidance, but he himself was in doubt about his own faith. He was not learned but had a unique character. He had a magnetic personality and attracted youth with felicity and elegance. From Anglican Church he moved to Roman Church after he gained a semblance of stable faith. His best writings besides essays are on theology. There is clear musical majesty in his writings in which he combined vital force with essential elegance.

In the essay he analyses the traits of a gentleman. A Gentleman is one who never inflicts pain on others, is refined, cultured and balanced. Above all, he is one who avoids controversies and treads a path of righteousness. It is interesting to note that Newman himelf was a person always involved in controversies.

References

Obstacles — hinderances or something in the way which either stops or makes any progress difficult.

Absurd — not sensible, unreasonable, funny.

Slander — a statement to harm or damage reputation.

Prudence — caution with regard to practical matters.

Bereavement — sorrow in death of someone close, to deprive ruthlessly by force.

Venerable — deserving respect due to position, age and qualities of character.

Effeminacy — the state or quality of being effeminate ie soft, delicate, unmanly.

Theological — a study of nature of God and foundation of religion.

Deductions — to conclude, to drive a conclusion from something known of assumed generally based on logic.

❑

OF UNITY IN RELIGION

FRANCIS BACON

Religion being the chief hand of human society, it is a happy thing when itself is well contained within the true band of unity. The quarrels and divisions about religion were evils unknown to the heathen. The reason was, because the religion of the heathen consisted rather in rites and ceremonies than in any constant belief. For you may imagine what kind of faith theirs was, when the chief doctors and fathers of their church were the poets. But the true God hath this attribute, that He is a jealous God; and therefore His worship and religion will endure no mixture nor partner. We shall therefore speak a few words concerning the Unity of the Church; what are the Fruits thereof; what the Bounds; and what the Means.

The Fruits of Unity (next unto the well-pleasing of God which is all in all) are two; the one towards those that are without the Church, the other towards those that are within. For the former; it is certain that heresies and schisms are of all others the greatest scandals, yea, more than corruption of manners. For as in the natural body a wound or solution of continuity is worse than a corrupt humour, so in the spiritual. So that nothing doth so much keep men out of the Church, and drive men out of the Church, as breach of unity. And therefore, whensoever it cometh to that pass that one saith, *Ecce in deserto,* another saith *Ecce* in *penetlabibus*—that is, when some men seek Christ in the conventicles of heretics, and others in an outward face of a Church—that voice had need continually to sound in men's ears, *Nolite exire.* The Doctor of the Gentiles (the propriety of whose vocation drew him to have a special care of those without) saith, *If a heathen come in, and hear you speak with several tongues, will he not say that you are mad ?* And certainly it is little better when atheists and profane persons do hear of so many discordant and contrary opinions in religion; it doth avert them from the Church, and maketh them to *sit down in the chair of the scorners.* It is a but a light thing to be vouched in so serious a matter, but yet it expresseth well the deformity; there is Master of scoffing, that in his catalogue of books of a feigned library, sets down this title of a book, *The Morris Dance of Heretics.*

For, indeed, every sect of them have a diverse posture, or cringe by themselves; which cannot but move derision in worldlings and depraved politics, who are apt to contemn holy things.

As for the Fruit towards those that are within, it is peace, which containeth infinite blessings. It establisheth faith; it kindleth charity; the outward peace of the Church distilleth into peace of conscience, and it turneth the labours of writing and reading controversies into treatises of mortification and devotion.

Concerning the Bonds of Unity, the true placing of them importeth exceedingly. There appear to be two extremes; for to certain zelants all speech of pacification is odious. *It is peace, Jehu ? What hast thou to do with peace ? Turn thee behind me.* Peace is not the matter, but following and party. Contrariwise, certain Laodiceans and lukewarm persons think they may accommodate points of religion by middle ways, and taking part of both, and witty reconcilements, as if they would-make an arbitrement between God and man. Both these extremes are to be avoided; which will done if the league of Christians, penned by our Saviour Himself, were in the two cross clauses thereof soundly and plainly expounded : *He that is not with us is against us;* and again, *He that is not us is with us : against* that is, if the fundamental, and of substance in religion, were truly discerned and distinguished from points not merely of faith, but of opinion, order, or good intention. This is a thing may seem to many a matter trivial, and done already : but if it were done less partially, it would be embraced more generally.

Of this I may give only this advice, according to my small model. Men ought to take heed of rending God's Church by two kinds of controversies. The one is, when the matter of the point controverted is too small and light, not worth the heat and strife about it, kindled only by contradiction. For, as it is noted by one of the fathers, *Christ coat indeed had no seam, but the Church's vesture was of divers colours;* whereupon he saith *In veste varietas sit, scissura non sit;* they be two things, Unity and Uniformity. The other is, when the matter of the point controverted is great, but it is driven to an over-great subtility and obscurity, so that it becometh a thing rather ingenious than substantial. A man that is of judgment and understanding shall sometimes hear ignorant men differ, and know well within himself that those which so differ mean one thing, and yet they themselves would never agree. And if it come so to pass in that distance of judgment which is between man and man, shall we not think that God above, that knows the heart, doth not discern that frail men, in some of their contradictions, intend the same thing, and accepteth of both ? The nature of such controversies is excellently expressed by St. Paul in the warning and precept that he giveth concerning the same, *Devita profaras vocum novitateset oppositions falsi nominis scientive.* Men create opposition which are not, and put them into new terms so fixed, as whereas the meaning ought to govern the term, the term in effect governeth the meaning. There be also two false Peaces, or Unities, the one, when the peace is grounded but upon an implicit ignorance (for all colours will agree in the dark); the other when it is pieced up upon a direct admission of contraries in fundamental points. For truth and falsehood in such things are like the iron and clay in the toes of Nebuchadnezzar's image : they may cleave but they will not incorporate.

Concerning the Means of procuring Unity, men must beware, that in the procuring or muniting of religious unity, they do not dissolve and deface the laws of charity and of human society. There be two swords, amongst Christians, the spiritual and the temporal, and both have their due office and place in the maintenance of religion. But we may not take up the third sword, which is Mahomet's sword, or like unto it—that is, to propagate religion by wars, or by sanguinary persecutions to force consciences (except it be in cases of overt scandal blaspheiny, or intermixture of practice against the state), much less to nourish seditions, to authorise conspiracies and rebellions, to put the sword into the people's hands, and the like, tending to the subversion of all government, which is the ordinance of God. For this is but to dash the first table against the second.

OF UNITY IN RELIGION

About the Author

Francis Bacon was born on January 22, 1561 in London. He came of an aristocratic family, being the son of Sir Nicholas Bacon, Lord Keeper of the Great-Seal. His mother was the daugher of Sir Anthony Cooke and Sister-in-law of Sir William Cecil (Lord Burghley).

In October 1620 he published **The Novum Organum** (or, The New Instrument for Interpretations of Nature and Discovery of Truth). This work elicited the warmest expressions of admiration from the ablest men of Europe. A further honour was conferred on him in Jan, 1621 when he was appointed viscount St. Albans. Bacon was now, at the summit of his career. He had won honours, dignities, wealth and public esteem. But his tenure in politics was not pure and he suffered disrepute even to the extent of being imprisoned for showing arbitrariness in his action of public importance.

The remaining five years of his life were spent in work far more valuable to the world than anything he had accomplished in his high office. From a literary and philosophical point of view, this last period was the most precious. Smitten by disgrace he turned with eagerness to intellectual pursuits that had been interrupted by his official duties. His new delight in his intellectual labours is finaly reflected in his essay **Of Nature in Men**. His retirement from politics enabled him, indeed to make his literary reputation more firm and enduring.

He devoted hismself with amazing energy to literature and science, and during this period produced his histories (**History of Henery** VII, **History of Great Britain** etc.) **De Augmentis** (Advancement of Learning), New Atlantis. Not the least important work is the final revision of his **Essays** numbering fifty eight. This was his last literary undertaking and was published a few months before his death on 9th April, 1626. The present essay is from this cluster of essays.

The central thought of this essay is, of course, that religious dissensions are harmful to faith, charity, and peace and should therefore be avoided. Bacon confines himself to the discussion of Christian religion. Bacon's advice is certainly of great value and can benefit people of other religion as well.

References

Band — bond, uniting force

Heresies and Schisms — a heresy means a belief which is opposed to one already established, and schism means a division or a rift.

Ecce in deseto — nehold He (Christ) is in the desert. This is a quotation from the gospel according to St. Metthew.

Ecce in penetralibus — 'behold he is in secret chambers'. Source is the same.

Conventicles of hereties — the religious meetings of the Dissenters or extreme protestants.

Nolite exise — 'go not forth'.

The Doctor of the Gentiles — St. Paul, who was sent to preach Christianity among the Gentiles or non-Jewish races.

Morris Dance — a dance popular in Elizabethan times.

Sanguinary Persecution — bloody methods of inflicting cruelty upon people holding different religious faith.

Ir a hominis non inplet justinium Dei — the wrath of man worketh not the righteousness of God.

❑

THE UNITY OF INDIAN CULTURE

HUMAYUN KABIR

Till recently the Aryans were regarded as the earliest invaders of the land. It was thought that they came to a country which was uncivilised and barbarian, but modern research has proved that there were invaders even before the Aryans poured into this land. They had evolved a civilisation higher than that of the Aryan hordes who came in their wake. These pre-Aryans had displaced still earlier people and built up a new civilisation which has astonished modern scholars by its extent and depth. The Aryan invasion repeated the process and led to fresh infusion of the old with the new. This continued with the successive inroads of fighting races who came to conquer but remained to lose themselves in the Indian racial cauldron. The Greek invaders were followed by Sakas and Huns and a hundred other nameless tribes. They all appeared on the scene as victors but were soon absorbed in the ranks of the vanquished.

Today whatever is India, whether it be an idea, a word, a form of art, a political institution or a social custom, is a blend of many different strains and elements.

In spite of this derivation from many sources and the consequent variety of forms and types, we find a remarkable unity of spirit informing Indian culture throughout the ages. In fact, it is this underlying unity which is one of the most remarkable features of Indian culture. In volume and duration no civilisation (with the possible exception of the Chinese) can bear comparison with the civilisation of India. The area of the land, the number of the people, the variety of the races and the length of India's history are hardly repeated elsewhere. The vitality of Indian culture is equally amazing. In spite of a thousand vicissitudes, it has survived to the modern day. This has been possible only on account of a sense of Indianness which imposed unity on all diversity and wove into one fabric of national life the many strands of different texture, colour and quality which have entered here.

The ancient world threw up fine flowers of civilisation in many lands.

With the exception of India and China, they are all dead and gone. It is only in India and to some extent in China that the old civilisation and culture have grown and changed, but never grown or changed at the expense of an underlying unity. This has been possible only through the capacity of readjustment exhibited by the Indian society.

One ground of this adjustment is found in the spirit of toleration that has characterised Indian history throughout the ages. "Live and let live" has been the policy of the Indians in all spheres of life. Sometimes this has been carried so far that contrary, if not contradictory, attitudes have been allowed to survive simultaneously. Toleration had led to the sufferance of evil and even to indifference to the values of life. This, however, is at worst the defect of a virtue. Such toleration is perhaps preferable to the fanatic devotion which leads to the denial and persecution of all other values but its own.

Throughout the changes of Indian history we therefore find a spirit of underlying unity which informs the diverse expressions of its life. But the unity was never a dead uniformity. A living unity never is.

Unity and universality must belong to any culture that is true and vital. Now, culture is a concept which cannot be simply or unitarily defined. There is no single character or mark which can be regarded as the essence or distinctive feature of culture. It is always a complex of many strands of varying importance and vitality. If we attempt to differentiate between culture and civilisation, we might say that civilisation is the organisation of life which makes civil society possible. Culture, on the other hand, is the resultant of such organisation and expresses itself through language and art, through philosophy and religion, through social habits and customs and through political institutions and economic organisations. Not one of them is separately culture, but collectively they constitute the expression of life which we describe as culture. Culture is the efflorescence of civilisation. Civilisation is the organisation of society which creates the condition of culture. There can, therefore, be no culture without civilisation, but there may be civilisations which have not yet developed their culture. Perhaps what is more often the case is that there are civilised people among whom only a small section have achieved culture. We have therefore had and still have races and nations that are civilised; but except for India, we have not yet had any nation or race that could be regarded as cultured in all its sections and classes, for here in India, culture is almost as extensive as civilisation itself.

The experience of European countries gives us cases of civilisation without culture. In India, on the other hand, even the casual tourist has observed that the difference between the masses and classes is not one of quality and can be explained in terms of information and opportunity. It is often otherwise in Europe. There the difference in quality between the masses and the classes is at times so great that it has shaken the faith of the most fervent of democrats.

The remarkable phenomenon can be explained only in terms of the unity and continuity of Indian culture. Unity is in one sense, the common characteristic of all culture. What specially distinguishes the culture of India is its unbroken continuity. Here, there have been no violent or sudden breaks, but on the contrary, a steady growth and expansion of culture which has gradually permeated every class and section of society.

UNITY OF INDIAN CULTURE

About the Author

Poet, Literateur, parliamentarian, educationist, was for sometime a member of the Union Cabinet as Minister for Scientific Research and Cultural Affairs. He was also associated with the publication of Maulana Azad's controversial book, **India Wins Freedom.** While at Oxford he was elected President of the Oxford University, a rare honour to any foreign student.

The unity of Indian culture is an adaptation of one of The Series of Lectures Humauan Kabir delivered in Baroda University. The culture of India, according to the author, is older than the beginning of human history. Modern research has revealed that. India had a well-developed culture even before the advent of the Aryans on the Indian Soil. There has been stratification of cultures in course of thousand of years and the culture of our country, as we have it today, is the result of fusions and blendings of different strands and events. It is a composite culture. There is a unity behind the apparent diversity of Indian culture. Indian culture alone has an unbroken continuity. It is vital, vibrant and great in the sense that it has the spirit of tolerance and in nature it is liberal. The present piece will help in understanding the integration of Indian culture.

Reference

Invaders — attackers of a country.

Barbarians — uncivilized savage

Hordes	— wandering tribes.
In the wake	— following them
Infusion	— mixing
Successive inroads	— attacks made one after another with a view to plundering.
Social cauldron	— a large, deep pan in which things are boiled and blended. The author means that different races got mixed up and were assimilated into one composite whole.
Huns	— a savage tribe that attacked Europe and India between the third and fifth century A.D.
Blend	— mixure.
Vicissitudes	— ups and downs.
Strands	— the threads twisted in making fabric.
Live and let lie	— the principle of co-existence
Sufference	— dislilked but not openly.
Indifference	— absence of interest.
Defect of a virtue	— when carried to an excess, a virtue becomes a defect.
Universality	— the quality of being comprehensive
Efflorescence	— a flowering, blooming.
Permeated	— passed through the pores of.

❑

TRUTH AND AHIMSA

MAHATMA GANDHI

It is not without a wrench that I have to take leave of the reader. I set a high value on my experiments. I do not know whether I have been able to do justice to them. I can only say that I have spared no pains to give a faithful narrative. The describe truth, as it has appeared to me, and in the exact manner in which I have arrived at it, has been my ceaseless effort. The exercise has given me ineffable mental peace, because it has been my fond hope that it might bring faith in Truth and Ahimsa to waverers.

My uniform experience convinced me that there is no other God than Truth. And if every page of these chapters does not proclaim to the reader that the only means for the realization of Truth is Ahimsa, I shall deem all my labour in writing these chapters to have been in vain. And, even though my efforts in this behalf may prove fruitless let the readers know that the vehicle, not the great principle, is at fault. After all, however sincere my strivings after Ahimsa may have been, they have still been imperfect and inadequate. The little fleeting glimpses, therefore, that I have been able to have of Truth can hardly convey an idea of the indescribable lustre of Truth, a million times more intense than that of the sun we daily see with our eyes. In fact what I have caught is only the faintest glimmer of that mighty effulgence. But this much I can say with assurance, as a result of all my experiments, that a perfect vision of Truth can only follow a complete realization of Ahimsa.

To see the universal and all-pervading Spirit of Truth face to face one must be able to love the meanest of creation as oneself. And a man who aspires after that cannot afford to keep out of any field of life. That is why my devotion to Truth has drawn me into the field of politics; and I can say without the slightest hesitation, and yet in all humility, that those who say that religion has nothing to do with politics do not know what religion means.

Identification with everything that lives is impossible without self-purification the observance of the law of Ahiṁsa must remain an empty dream. God can never be realized by one who is not pure of heart. Self-purification therefore must mean purification in all the walks of life. And purification being highly infections, purification of oneself necessarily leads to the purification of one's surroundings.

But the path of self-purification is hard and steep. The attain to perfect purity one has to become absolutely passion-free in thought, speech and action, to rise above the opposing currents of love and hatred, attachment and repulsion. I know that I have not in me as yet that triple purity, in spite of constant, ceaseless striving for it. That is why the world's praise fails to move me, indeed it very often stings me. To conquer the subtle passions seems to me to be harder far than the physical conquest of the world by the force of arms. Ever since my return to India I have had experiences of the dormant passions lying hidden within me. The knowledge of them has made me feel humiliated though not defeated. The experiences and experiments have sustained me and given me great joy. But I know that I have still before me a difficult path to traverse. I must reduce myself to zero. So long as a man does not act of his own free will, put himself last among his fellow creatures, there is no salvation for him. Ahimsa is the farthest limit of humility.

In bidding farewell to the reader, for the time being at any rate, I ask him to join with me in prayer to the God of Truth that He may grant me the boon of Ahimsa in mind, word and deed.

TRUTH AND AHIMSA

About the Author

Mohandas Karamachand Gandhi (1869-1948), commonly known as Mahatma Gandhi was supposedly the greatest Indian revolutionary, political leader, statesman and social reformer of modern India. He spiritualized the political life of India by adopting non-violence and truth as the only means of attaining India's freedom. In addition to his struggle for freedom from the British rule, he launched various movements such as Hindu-Muslim Unity, upliftment of the untouchables, revival of cottage industries, basic education and propagation of Khadi to name only a few. He is remembered and respected as 'Father of the Nation'. A man of exceptional literary talent Mahatma Gandhi was a versatile genius. His prose style has a rare grace, simplicity and felicity of expression. He makes no attempt at decorating his language by rehetorical devices. His style has the Biblical simplicity which goes straight to the heart of the readers. His autobiography, **The Story of My Experiments with Truth** is a great classic in Indian English literature. His essays and speeches are equally illuminating, informative and instructive.

'Truth and Ahimsa' is an extract from Mahatma Gandhi's autobiography **'The Story of My Experiments with Truth.** Here he points out the importance of Truth and Ahimsa. He is convinced that there is no other God than Truth. A perfect vision of Truth can only follow a complete realization of Ahimsa. One must be able to love others as oneself. This is possible only through self purification. One must be pure at heart in order to obey the laws of Ahimsa. Self purification is needed on three levels, purity in thought, speech and action. Perfect purify is a state of attainment of passion-free life. Ahimsa is the farthest limit of humility. By following Ahimsa in mind, word and deed one can have realisation of Truth.

References

My experiments — experiments described by Gandhiji in his auto-biography.

Difficult path to traverse — a faith which is full of difficulties.

Ineffable — unspeakable.

Waverers — one who has unsettled opinons.

Effulgence — great lustre or radiance.

❑

THE SECRET OF WORK

SWAMI VIVEKANANDA

The miseries of the world cannot be cured by physical help only. Until man's nature changes, his physical needs will always arise, and miseries will always be felt, and no amount of physical help will remove them completely. The only solution of the problem is to make mankind pure. Ignorance is the mother of evil and of all the misery we see. Let men have light, let them be pure and spiritually strong and educated; then alone will misery cease in the world. We may convert every house in the country into a charitable asylum; we may fill the land with hospitals, but human misery will continue until man's character changes.

We read in the *Bhagawad Geeta* again and again that we must all work incessantly. We cannot do any work which will not do some good somewhere; there cannot also be any work which will not cause some harm somewhere. Every work must necessarily be a mixture of good and evil; yet we are commanded to work incessantly. Good and evil will both have their consequences. Good action will entail upon us good effect; bad action bad. But good and bad both forge fetters for the soul. The solution reached in the *Geeta* in regard to this cramping influence of work is, that if we do not attach ourselves to it, it will not hold our soul in bondage.

This is the one central idea in the *Geeta;* work incessantly, but be not attached to it. To use the simile of a lake for the mind, no ripple or wave that rises in it, dies out entirely, but it leaves a mark and there is a possibility of that wave coming out again. This mark, with the possibility of the wave reappearing, is what is called *Samskara.* Every work that we do, every movement of the body, every thought that we think, leaves such an impression on the mind-stuff, and even when the impressions are not obvious on the surface, they work in the subconscious region of the brain. What we are is determined every moment by the sum total of these impressions on the mind. What I am just at this moment, is the effect of the sum total of all the impressions of my past life. This is really what is meant by character; each man's character is determined by the sum total of these impressions. If good impressions prevail, the character becomes good; if bad, it becomes bad. If a man continuously hears bad words, thinks bad thoughts, does bad acts, his mind will be full of bad impressions; and they will influence his thought and work without his being conscious of the fact. These bad impressions will always be working, and their resultant must be evil, and the man will be a bad man : he cannot help it. The sum total of these impressions in him will create a strong motive power for doing bad acts. He will be like a machine in the hands of his impressions, and they will force him to do evil. Similarly, if a man thinks good thoughts and does good work, the sum total of their impressions will be good; and this, in a similar manner, will force him to do good even in spite of himself. When a man has done so much good work and thought so many good thoughts that there is an irresistible tendency in him to do good in spite of himself and even if he wishes to do evil, his mind, as the sum total of his tendencies, will not allow him do so; these will hold him back. When such is the case, the man's good character is said to be established.

As the tortoise tucks its feet and head inside the shell and will not come out even though you may break the shell into pieces, even so the character of the man who has control over his motives and organs, is unchangeably established. He controls his own inner forces, and nothing can draw them out against his will. By this continuous reflex of good thoughts and good impressions moving over the surface of the mind, the tendency to do good becomes strong, and in consequence we are able to control the *Indriyas* (sense-organs, the nerve-centres). Thus alone is character formed, and only a man of character can get at truth. Such a man is safe for ever; he cannot do any evil. You may place him in any company, but there will be no danger for him. There is a still higher state than having this good tendency, and that is the desire for liberation. Liberation means full freedom—freedom from the bondage of good, as well as from the bondage of evil. A golden chain is as much a chain as an iron one. There is a thron in my finger, and I use another to take the first one out, and when I have taken it out, I throw both of them aside. I have no necessity for keeping the second thorn, because it is a thorn after all. So bad tendencies are to be counteracted by good ones, and bad impressions on the mind should be removed by the fresh waves of good ones, until all that is evil almost disappears, or is subdued and held in control in a corner of the mind; but after that the good tendencies also have to be removed. Thus the 'attached' becomes the 'unattached'. Work, but let not the action or the thought produce a deep impression on your mind. Let the ripples come and go, let great actions proceed from the muscles and the brain, but let them not make any deep impression on the soul.

How can this be done ? We see that the impression of every action to which we get attached remains. I may meet hundreds of persons during they day, and among them meet also one whom I love; but when I retire at night and try to think of all the faces I saw, only one face comes before the mind's eye—the face which I saw perhaps only for one minute and which I loved, all the others have vanished. Owing to my attachment to a particular person, his face caused a deep impression on my mind than those of the others. But physically, the impressions have all been the same.

Therefore, he 'unattached', yet the brain-centres work; work incessantly, but let not the mind be affected. Work as if you were a stranger in this land, a sojourner; work incessantly, but do not bind yourselves; bondage is terrible. This world is not our habitation, it is only one of the many stages through which we are passing.

The gist of this teaching is that you should work like a master and not like a slave; work incessantly, but do not do slave's work. Do you not see how everybody works ? Nobody can be altogether at rest; ninety-nine per cent of men work like slaves, and the result is misery; it is all selfish work. But work with freedom, inspired by love ! There is no true love possible in the slave. If you buy a slave and tie him down in chains and make him work for you, he will work like a drudge, but there will be no love in him. So when we ourselves work for the things of the world as slaves, there can be no love in us, and work is not true work. This is true of work done for relatives and friends, and is true of work done for ourselves. Selfish work is slave's work; and here is a test. Every act of love brings happiness; there is no act of love which does not bring peace and blessedness in its train. Real existence, real knowledge, and real love are eternally connected with one another, the three in one; where one of them is, the others also must be; they are the three aspects of the One without a second—the Existence-Knowledge-Bliss.

Krishna says—'Look at me, Arjuna ! If I stop from work for one moment, the whole universe will decay. I have nothing to gain from work : I am the one Lord, but why do I work ? Because I love the world." God is unattached because he loves; real love makes us unattached.

To attain this unattachment is almost a life's work, but as soon as we have reached this point, we have attained the goal of love and become free; the bondage of nature falls from us, and we see nature as she is.

Do you ask anything of your children in return for what you have given them ? It is your duty to work for them, and there the matter ends. In whatever you do for a particular person, a city, or a state, assume the same attitude towards it as you have towards your children—expect nothing in return. If you can invariably take the position of a giver, in which everything given by you is a free offering to the world, without any thought of return, your work will bring you no attachment. Attachment comes only where we expect a return.

If working like slaves results in selfish attachment, working as masters of our own mind gives rise to the bliss of non-attachment. We often talk of right and justice, but we find that in this world right and justice are mere baby's talk. There are two things which guide the conduct of men : might and mercy. The exercise of might is invariably an act of selfishness. All men and women try to make the most of whatever power or advantage they have. Mercy is heavenly, to be good, we have all to be merciful. Even justice and right should stand on mercy. All thought of obtaining return for the work we do, hinders our spiritual progress; nay, in the end it brings misery. There is another way in which this idea of mercy and selfless charity can be put into practice, that is, by looking upon work as 'worship', Here we give up all the fruits of our work unto the Lord, and, worshipping Him thus, we have no right to expect anything from mankind for what we do. The Lord Himself works incessantly and is ever without attachment. Just as water cannot wet the lotus leaf, so work cannot bind the unselfish man by giving rise to attachment to results. The selfless and unattached man may live in the very heart of a crowded and sinful city, yet he will not be touched by sin.

THE SECRET OF WORK

About the Author

Swami Vivekanand (1863-1902) is a memorable name in Indian History. He is one of the makers of modern India. His first name was Narendranath Dutt, but he became Vivekanand after he joined the Ashram of Ramkrishna Paramhans. He became his disciple after having been convinced of his spiritual powers. In his short span of life, he toured extensively in India and abroad and delivered scores of lectures in order to propogate the ideals of his teacher. He was, perhaps, the first Indian to raise his country and its culture in the eyes of the west. His lectures and writings possess a clarity and force which comes not only from the mastery of the language but also from his total commitment to the cause he was working for.

The Secret of Work is an extract from **Karma Yoga** a part of **Bhagawad Geeta**. Swami Vivekanand gives a remarkable exposition of the idea of non-attachment to action. **The Geeta** says 'work incessantly, but be not attached to it ? 'Bondage, according to him is terrible'. Work like a master and not like a slave.

References

Miseries — great sufferings

Pure — free from sin.

Charitable asylum — a free place for rest and recuperation.

Entail — impose

Forge fetters — make chains

Sojourner — one who stays for a short time.

Drudge — to work hard at unpleasant tasks.

Arjuna — one of the five Pandavas.

Universe — the world

Bondage — not free.

❑

LIFE'S PHILOSOPHY

JAWAHARLAL NEHRU

Six or seven years ago an American publisher asked me to write an essay on my philosophy of life for a symposium he was preparing. I was attracted to the idea but I hesitated, and the more I thought over it, the more reluctant I grew. Ultimately I did not write that essay.

What was my philosophy of life ? I did not know. Some years earlier I would not have been so hesitant. There was a definiteness about my thinking and objectives then which has faded away since. The events of the past few years in India, China, Europe and all over the world have been confusing, upsetting and distressing, and the future has become vague and shadowy and has lost that clearness of outline which it once possessed in my mind.

This doubt and difficulty about fundamental matters did not come in my way in regard to immediate action, except that it blunted somewhat the sharp edge of that activity. No longer could I function, as I did in my younger days, as an arrow flying automatically to the target of my choice, ignoring all else but that target. Yet I functioned, for the urge to action was there and a real or imagined coordination of that action with the ideals I held. But a growing distaste for politics, as I saw them, seized me and gradually me whole attitude to life seemed to undergo a transformation.

The ideals and objectives of yesterday were still the ideals of today but they had lost some of their lustre, and even as one seemed to go towards them, they lost the shining beauty which had warmed the heart and vitalized the body. Evil triumphed often enough, but what was far worse was the coarsening and distortion of what had seemed so right. Was human nature so essentially bad that it would take ages of training, though suffering and misfortune, before it could behave reasonably and raise man above that creature of lust and violence and deceit that he now was ? And meanwhile was every effort to change it radically in the present or the near future doomed to failure ?

Ends and means : were they tied up inseparably, acting and reacting on each other, the wrong meand distorting and sometimes even destroying the end in view ? But the right means might well be beyond the capacity of infirm and selfish human naute. What then was one to do ? Not to act was a a complete confession of failure and a submission to evil; to act meant often enough a compromise with some form of that evil, with all the untoward consequences that such compromises result in.

My early approach to life's problems had been more or less scientific, with something of the easy optimism of the sience of the nineteenth and early twentieth century. A secure and comfortable existence, and the energy and self-confidence I possessed, increased that feeling of optimism. A kind of vague humanism appealed to me.

Religion as I saw it practised, and accepted even by thinking minds, whether it was Hinduism or Islam or Buddhism or Christianity, did not attract me. It seemed to be closely associated with superstitious practices and dogmatic beliefs, and behind it lay a method of approach to life's problems which was certainly not that of science. There was an element of magic about it, an uncritical credulousness a reliance on the supernatural.

Yet is was obvious that religion had supplied some deeply felt inner need of human nature, and that the vast majority of people all over the world could not do without some form of religious belief. It had produced many fine types of men and women, as well as bigoted, narrow-minded, cruel tyrants. It had given a set of values to human life, and though some of these values had no application today, or were even harmful, others were still the foundation of morality and ethics.

In the wider sense of the word, religion dealt with the uncharted regions of human experience; uncharted, that is, by the scientific positive knowledge of the day. In a sense it might be considered an extension of the known and charted region, though the methods of science and religion were utterly unlike each other, and to a large extent they had to deal with different kinds of media. It was obvious that there was a vast unknown region all around us and science, with its magnificant achievements, knew little enough about it, though it was making tentative approaches in that direction. Probably also the normal methods of science, its dealings with the visible world and the processes of life, were not wholly adapted to the psychical, the artistic, the spiritual, and other elements of the invisible world. Life does not consist entirely of what we see and hear and feel, the visible world which is undergoing change in time and space. It is continually touching an invisible world of ether, and possible more stable or equally changeable elements; and no thinking person can ignore this invisible world.

Science does not tell us much, or for the matter of that anything, about the purpose of life. It is now widening its boundaries and it may invade the so-called invisible world before long and help us to understand this purpose of life in its widest sense, or at leaast give us some glimpses which illumine the problem of human existence. The old controversy between science and religion takes a new form—the application of the scientific method to emotional and religious experiences.

Religion merges into mysticism and metaphysics and philosophy. There have been great mystics, attractive figures, who cannot easily be disposed of as self-deluded fools. Yet mysticism (in the narrow sense of the word) irritates me; it appears to be vague and soft and flabby, not a rigorous discipline of the mind but a surrender of mental faculties and a living in a sea of emotional experience. The experience may lead occasionally to some insight into inner and less obvious processes, but it is also likely to lead to self-delusion.

Metaphysics and philosophy, or a metaphysical philosophy, have a greater appeal to the mind. They require hard thinking and the application of logic and reasoning, though all this is necessarily based on some premises, which are presumed to be self-evident and yet which may or may not be true. All thinking persons to a greater or less degree, dabble in metaphysics and philosophy, for not to do so is to ignore many of the aspects of this universe of ours. Some may feel more attracted to them than others, and the emphasis on them may vary in different ages. In the ancient world both in Asia and Europe, all the emphasis was laid on the supremacy of the inward life over things external and this inevitably led to metaphysics and philosophy. The modern man is wrapped up much more in these external things, and yet even he, in moments of crisis and mental trouble, often turns to philosophy and metaphysical speculations.

Some vague or more precise philosophy of life we all have, though most of us accept unthinkingly the general attitude which is characteristic of our generation and environment. Most of us accept also certain metaphysical conceptions as part of the faith in which we have grown up. I have not been attracted towards metaphysics; in fact I have had a certain distaste for vague speculation. And yet I have sometimes found a certain intellectual fascination in trying to follow the rigid lines of metaphysical and philosophic thought of thc ancients or the moderns. But I have never felt at ease there and have escaped from their spell with a feeling of relief.

Essentially I am interested in this world, in this life, not in some other world or a future life. Whether there is such a thing as a soul, or whether there is a survival after death or not, I do not know; and important as these questions are, they do not trouble me in the least. They environment in which I have grown up takes the soul (or rather the *atma*) and a future life, the *Karma* theory of cause and effect, and reincarnation for ganted. I have been affected by this and so, in a sense, I am favourably disposed towards these assumptions. There might be a soul which survives the physical death of the body, and a theory of cause and effect governing life's actions seems reasonable though it leads to obvious difficulties when one thinks of the ultimate cause. Presuming a soul, there appears to be some logic also in the theory of reincarnation.

But I do not believe in any of these or other theories and assumptions as a matter of religious faith. They are just intellectual speculations in an unknown region about which we know next to nothing. They do not affect my life, and whether they were proved right or wrong subsequently, they would make little difference to me.

Spiritualism with its seances and its so-called manifestations of spirits and the like has always seemed to me a rather absurd and impertinent way of investigating psychic phenomena and the mysteries of the after-life. Usually it is something worse and is an exploitation of the emotions of some over-credulous people who seek relief or escape from mental trouble. I doe not deny the possibility of some of these psychic phenomena having a basis of truth, but the approach appears to me to be all wrong and the conclusions drawn from scraps and odd bits of evidence to be unjustified.

Often, as I look at this world, I have a sense of mysteries of unknown depths. The urge to understand, it, in so far as I can, comes to me; to be in tune with it and to experience it in its fullness. But the way to that understanding seems to me essentially the way of science, the way of objective approach, though I realized that there can be no such thing as true objectiveness. If the subjective element is unavoidable and inevitable, it should be conditioned as far as possible by the scientifc method.

What the mysterious is I do not know. I do not call it God because God has come to mean much that I do not believe in. I find myself incapable of thinking of a deity or of any unknown supreme power in anthropomorphic terms, and the fact that many people think so is continually a source of surprise to me. Any idea of a personal God seems very odd to me. Intellectually, I can appreciate to some extent the conception of monism, and I have been attracted towards the *Advaita* (non-dualist) philosophy of the Vedanta, though I do not presume to understand it in all its depth and intricacy, and I realize that merely an intellectual appreciation of such matters does not carry one far. At the same time the Vedanta, as well as other similar approaches, rather frighten me with their vague formless incursions into infinity. The diversity and fullness of nature stir me and produce a harmony of the spirit, and I can imagine myself feeling at home in the old Indian or Greek pagan and pantheistic atmosphere, but minus the conception of God or gods that was attached to it.

Some kind of ethical approach to life has a strong appeal for me, though it would be difficult for me to justify it logically. I have been attracted by Gandhiji's stress on right means and I think one of his greatest contributions to our public life has been this emphasis. The idea is by no means new, but this application of an ethical doctrine to large-scale public activity was certainly novel. It is full of difficulty, and perhaps ends and means are not really separable and form together one organic whole. In a world which thinks almost exclusively of ends and ignores means, the emphasis on means seems odd and remarkable. How far it has succeeded in India I cannot say. But there is no doubt that it has created a deep and abiding impression on the minds of large numbers of people.

A study of Marx and Lenin produced a powerful effect on my mind and helped me to see history and current affairs in a new light. The long chain of history and of social development appeared to have some meaning, some sequence, and the future lost some of its obscurity. The practical achievements of the Soviet Union were also tremendously impressive. Often I disliked or did not understand some development there and it seemed to me to be too closely concerned with the opportunism of the moment or the power politics of the day. But despite all these developments and possible distortions of the original passion for human betterment, I had no doubt that the Soviet Revolution had advanced human society by a great leap and had lit a bright flame which could not be smothered and that it had laid the foundations for the 'new civilization' towards which the world would advnace. I am too much of individualist and believer in personal freedom to like overmuch regimentation. Yet it seemed to me obvious that in a complex social structure individual freedom had to be limited, and perhaps the only way to real personal freedom was though some such limitation in the social sphere. The lesser liberties may often need limitation in the interest of the larger freedom.

Much in the Marxist philosophical outlook I could accept without difficulty; its monism and non-duality of mind and matter, the dynamics of matter and the dialectic of continuous change by evolution as well as leap, through action and interaction, cause and effect, thesis, antithesis and synthesis. It did not satisfy me completely, nor did it naswer all the questions in my mind, and almost unawares a vague idealist approach would creep into my mind, something rather akin to the Vedanta approach. It was not a difference between mind and matter but rather of something that lay beyond the mind. Also there was the background of ethics. I realized that the moral approach is a changing one and depends upon the growing mind and an advancing civilization; it is conditioned by the mental climate of the age. Yet there was something more to it than that, certain basic urges which had greater performanence. I did not like the frequent divorce in communist, as in other, practice between action and these basic urges or principles. So there was an odd mixture in my , mind which I could not rationally explain or resolve. There was a general tendency not to think too much of those fundamental questions which appear to be beyond reach, and rather to concentrate on the problems of life—to understand in the narrower and more immediate sense what should be done and how. Whatever ultimate reality may be, and whether we can ever grasp it in whole or in part, there certainly appear to be vast possibilities of increasing human knowledge, even though this may be partly or largely subjective, and of applying this to the advancement and betterment of human living and social organization.

There has been in the past and there is to a lesser extent even today among some people, an absorption in finding an answer to the riddle of the universe. Thise leads them away from the individual and social problems of the day, and when they are unable to solve that riddle they despair and turn to inaction and triviality, or find comfort in some dogmatic creed. Social evils, most of which are certainly capable of removal, are attributed to original sin, to the unalterableness of 'human nature', or the social structure, or (in India) to the inevitable legacy of previous births. Thus one drifts away from even the attempt to think rationally and scientifically and takes refuge in irrationalism, superstition, and unreasonable and inequitable social prejudices and practices, It is true that even rational and scientific thought does not always take us as far as we would like to go. There is an infinite number of factors and relations which influence and determine events in varying degrees and it is impossible to grasp all of them. Still we can try to pick out the dominating forces at work and by observing external material reality, and by experiment and practice, trial and error, grope our way to ever-widening knowledge and truth.

For this purpose, and within these limitations the general Marxist approach, fitting in as it more or less did with the present state of scientific knowledge, seemed to me to offer considerable help. But even accepting that appraoch, the consequences that flow from it and the interpretation on past and present happenings were by no means always clear. Marx's general analysis of social development seems to have been remarkably correct, and yet many developments took place later which did not fit in with his outlook for the immediate future. Lenin successfully adapted the Marxian thesis to some of these subsequent developments, and again since then further remarkable changes have taken place—the rise of fascism and nazism and all that lay behind them. The very rapid growth of technology and the practical application of vast developments in scientific knowledge are now changing the world picture with an amazing rapidity, leading to new problems.

And so while I accepted the fundamentals of the socialist theory, I did not trouble myself about its numerous inner controversies. I had little patience with leftist groups in India, spending much of their energy in mutual conflict and recrimination over fine points of doctrine which did not interest me at all. Life is too complicated and, as far as we can understand it in our present state of knowledge, too illogical for it to be confined within the four corners of a fixed doctrine.

The real problems for me remain problems of individual and social life, of harmonious living, of a proper balancing of an individual's inner and outer life, of an adjustment of the relations between individuals and between groups, of a continuous becoming something better and higher, of social development, of the ceaseless advanture of man. In the solution of these problems the way of observation and precise knowledge and deliberate reasoning, according to the method of science, must be followed. This method may not always be applicable in our quest of truth, for art and poetry and certain psychic experiences seem to belong to a different order of things and to elude the objective methods of science. Let us therefore not rule out intuition and other methods of sensing truth and reality. They are necessary even for the purposes of science. But always we must hold to our anchor of precise objective knowledge tested by reason and even more so by experiment and practice, and always we must beware of losing ourselves in a sea of speculation unconnected with the day-to-day problems of life and the needs of men and women. A living philosophy must answer the problems of today.

It may be that we of this modern age, who so pride ourselves in the achievements of our times, are prisoners of our age just as the ancients and the men and women of medieval times were prisoners of their respective ages. We may delude ourselves, as others have done before us, that our way of looking at things is the only right way, leading to truth. We cannot escape from that prison or get rid entirely of that illusion, if illusion it is.

Yet, I am convinced that the methods and approach of science have revolutionized human life more than anything else in the long course of history, and have opened doors and avenues of further and even more radical change, leading up to the very portals of what has long been considered the unknown. The technical achievements of science are obvious enough, its capacity to transform an economy of scarcity into one of abundance is evident, its invasion of many problems which have so far been the monopoly of philosophy is becoming more pronounced. Space-time and the quantum theory utterly changed the picture of the physical world. More recent researches into the nature of matter, the structure of the atom, the transmutation of the elements, and the transformation of electricity and light, either into the other, have carried human knowledge much further. Man no longer sees nature as something apart and distinct from himself. Human destiny appears to become a part of nature's rhythmic energy.

All this upheaval of thought, due to the advance of science, has led scientists into a new region, verging on the metaphysical. They draw different and often contradictory conclusions. Some see in it a new unity, the antithesis of chance. Others, like Bertrand Russell, say : 'Academic philosophers ever since the time of Parmenides have believed the world is unity. The most fundamental of my beliefs is that this is rubbish.' Or again : 'Man is the product of causes which had no prevision of the end they were achieving; his origin, his growth, his hopes and fears, his loves and beliefs are but the outcome of accidental colloction of atoms.' And yet the latest developments in physics have gone a long way to demonstrate a fundamental unity in nature. 'The belief that all things are made of a single substance is as old as thought itself; but ours is the generation which, first of all in history, is able to perceive the unity of Nature not as a baseless dogma or a hopeless aspiration, but a principle of science based on proof as sharp and clear as anything which is known.'

Old as this belief is in Asia and Europe, it is interesting to compare some of the latest conclusions of science with the fundamental ideas underlying the *Advaita* Vedantic theory. These ideas were that the universe is made of one substance whose form is perpetually chaning, and further that the sum-total of energies remains always the same. Also that the 'explanations of things are to be found within their own nature, and that no external beings or existences are required to explain what is going on in the universe', with its corollary of a self-evolving universe.

It does not very much matter to science what these vague speculations lead to, for meanwhile it forges ahead in a hundred directions, in its own precise experimental way of observation, widening the bounds of the charted region of knowledge, and changing human life in the process. It may be on the verge of discovering vital mysteries, and yet they may elude it. Still it will go on along its appointed path for there is no end to its journeying. Ignoring for the moment the *why* of philosophy, it will go on asking *how*, and as it finds this out it gives greater content and meaning to life, and perhaps takes us some way to answering the *why*.

Or, perhaps, we cannot cross that barrier, and the mysterious will continue to remain the mysterious and life with all its changes will still remain a bundle of good and evil a succession of conflicts, a curious combination of incompatible and mutually hostile urges.

Or again, perhaps, the very progress of science, unconnected with and isolated from moral discipline and ethical considerations will lead to the concentration of power and the terrible instruments of detruction which it had made, in the hands of evil and selfish men, seeking the domination of others—and thus to the destruction of its own great achievements. Something of this kind we see happening now, and behind this war there lies this internal conflict of the spirit of man.

How amazing is this spirit of man ! In spite of innumerable failings, man, throughtout the ages, has sacrificed his life and all he held dear for an ideal, for truth, for faith, for country and honour. That ideal may change but that capacity for self-sacrifice continues, and, because of that, much may be forgiven to man, and it is impossible to lose hope for him. In the midst of disaster, he has not lost his dignity or his faith in the values he cherished. Play-things of Nature's mighty forces, less than a speak of dust in this vast universe, he has hurled defiance at the elemental powers, and with his mind, cradle of revolution, sought to master them. Whatever gods there be, there is something godlike in man, as there is also something of the devil in him.

The future is dark, uncertain. But we can see part of the way leading to it and can tread it with firm steps, remembering that nothing that can happen is likely to overcome the spirit of man which has survived so many perils. Remembering also that life, for all its ills, has joy and beauty, and we can always wander, if we know how to, in the enchanted woods of nature.

What else is Wisdom ? What of man's endeavour.
Or God's high grace, so lovely and so great ?
To stand from fear set free, to breathe and wait;
To hold a hand uplifted over Hate;
And shall not loveliness be loved for ever ?

LIFE'S PHILOSOPHY

About the Author

Jawaharlal Nehru (1889-1964) an Indian statesman was also a significant writer. He went to Harrow and Cambridge and was well versed with western thought, history, culture and way of life. In the freedom struggle with Gandhi as path-breaker he devoted his life to the cause of nation. Even after Independence in 1947 he went on friendly terms with the British and as the first Prime Minsiter he joined the Commonwealth of nations. In the days of cold war between the Western capitalist bloc and Eastern communist bloc he remained non-alligned with other Asean Nations. He wrote **Discovery of India** and **Glimpses of World History** besides many essays, letters and speeches.

The prose piece has been taken from **Discovery of India**. It was written during his stay in Aga Khan Palace where he was put in jail after Quit India Movement in 1942. This semi-historic work lets one see the great mind of the Western-educated freedom fighter and the first Prime Minister of India. In it he forges the links of racial memory and finally turns towards future. The quest-the thrilling voyage of discovery-the deserts, the oases, the hills, the streams, the mountain tops, the hidden vastness, the clash of races, rise and fall of civilizations present a kaliedoscopic world-view. The book has intensity of conviction and naturalness and beauty of expression. His belief in scientific-humanism was his driving motivation even later in life. His philospophy of life encompases the variety of experience and exposure. He was truly the citizen of world, and a great statesman with a vision of whom India is proud of. Religion never drew him and he developed the philosophy of secularism which has reflections of Marxian philosophy. He believed in the present and valued **Karma**. Knowledge could open new vistas if tempered with humanistic philosophy so he believed. He was amazed by the spirit of man. In spite of innumerable failings man throughout the ages has sacrificed his life and all that he held dear for an ideal, for truth, for faith. Even in the midst of disaster he has not lost his dignity or his faith. He may be a plaything of Nature's mighty forces but with his unsurmountable mind he can master it. This is his philosophy of life.

References

Blunted — having a dull edge,

Lusture — shine

Distortion — misrepresent

Metaphysics — branch of philosophy which deals with the ultimate nature of existence, reality and experience.

Anthropomorphic — resembling a human form

Upheaval — violent change or disturbance in society.

Hurled — to throw

Enchanted — bewitiched, magical influence.

❑

THE VARIETY AND UNITY OF INDIA

JAWAHARLAL NEHRU

The diversity of India is tremendous; it is obvious, it lies on the surface and anybody can see it. It concerns itself with physical appearence as well as with certain mental habits and traits. There is little in common, to outward seeming, between the Pathan of the North-West and the Tamil in the far South. Their racial stocks are not the same, though there may be common strands running through them; they differ in face and figure, food and clothing, and of course, language. In the North-West Frontier Province there is already the breath of Central Asia, and many a custom there, as in Kashmir, reminds one of the countries on the other side of the Himalayas. Pathan popular dances are singularly like Russian Cossak dancing. Yet with all these differences there is no mistaking the impress of India on the Pathan, as this is obvious in the Tamil. This is not surprising, for these border lands, and indeed Afghanistan also were united with India for thousands of years. The old Turkish and other races who inhabited Afghanistan and parts of Central Asia before the advent of Islam were largely Budhists, and earlier still, during the period of the Epics, Hindus. The frontier area was one of the principal centres of old Indian culture and it abounds still with ruins of monuments and monasteries and, specially, of the great university of Taxila, which was at the height of its fame two housand years ago, attracting students from all over India as well as different parts of Asia. Changes of religion made a difference but could not change entirely the mental backgrounds which the people of those are had developed.

The Pathan and the Tamil are two extreme examples; the others lie somewhere in between. All of them have their distinctive features, all of them have still more the distinguishing mark of India. It is fascinating to find how the Bengalees, the Marathas, the Gujratis, the Tamils, the Andhras, the Oriyas, the Assamese, the Canarese, the Malayalis, the Sindhis, the Punjabis, the Pathans, the Kashmiris, the Rajupts and the great central block comprising the Hindustani speaking people, have retained their peculiar characteristics for hundreds of years, have still more or less the same virtues and failings of which old tradtion or record tells us, and yet have been throughout these ages distincitively Indian, with the same national herit age and the same set of moral and mental qualities. There was something living and dynamics about this herit age which showed itself in ways of living and a philosophical attitude to life and its problems. Ancient India, like ancient China, was a world in itself, a culture and a civilization which gave shape to all things. Foreign influences poured in and often influenced that culture and were absorbed. Disruptive tendencies gave rise immediately to an attempt to find a synthesis. Some kind of a dream of unity has occupied the mind of India since the dawn of civilisation. That unity was not conceived as somthing imposed from outside, a standardization of externals of even of beliefs. It was something deeper and, within its fold the widest tolerance of belief and custom was practised and every variety acknowledged and even encouraged.

Differences, big or small can always be noticed even within a national group, however closely bound together it may be. The essential unity of that group becomes apparent when it is compared to another national group, though often the differences between two adjoining groups fade out or intermingle near the frontiers, and modern developments are tending to produce a certain uniformity everywhere. In ancient and medieval times, the idea of the modern nation was non-existent and feudal, religious, racial or cultural bonds, had more improtance. Yet I think that at almost any time in recorded history an Indian would have felt more or less at home in any part of India, and would have felt as a stranger and alien in any other country. He would certainly have felt less of a stranger in countries which had partly adopted his culture or religion. Those who professed a religion of non-Indian origin and coming to India settled down there, become distinctively Indian in the course of a few generations, such as Christians, Jews, Parsis, Moslems; Indiam converts to some of these religions never ceased to be Indians in spite of a change of faith. All these were looked upon in other countries as Indians and foreigners, even though there might have been a community of faith between them.

Today, when the conception of nationalism has developed much more, Indians in foreign countries inevitably form a national group and hang together for various purposes, in spite of their internal differences. An Indian Christian in looked upon as an Indian wherever he may go. An Indian Moslem is considered an Indian in Turkey or Arabia or Iran or any other country where Islam is the dominant religion.

All of us, I suppose, have varying pictures of our native land and no two persons will think exactly alike. When I think of India, I think of many things; of broad fields dotted with innumerable small villages; of towns and cities I have visited; of the magic of the rainy season which pours life into dry parched-up land and converts it suddenly into a glistening expanse of beauty and greenery, of great rivers and flowing water; of the Khyber Pass in all its bleak surroundings; of the southern tip of India; of people, individually and in the mass; and, above all, of the Himalayas, snow capped, or some mountain valley in Kashmir in the spring covered with new flowers, and with a brook bubbling and gurgling through it. We make and preserve the pictures of our choice, and so I have chosen this mountain background rather than the more normal picture of a hot, sub-tropical country. Both pictures would be correct for India stretches from the tropics right up to the temperate regions, from near the equator to the cold heart of Asia.

THE VARIETY AND UNITY OF INDIA

About the Author

Jawaharlal Nehru (1889-1964) was a freedom fighter, a great stateman and the first Prime Minister of Independent India. He had his schooling at Harrow and went for higher education at Cambridge. He was well versed in western thought but at the same time he was deeply versed in Indian ancient history and the emergence of a new India. He was committed to the cause of the nation. In his writings and action one can see the amalgamation of the East and the West tempered with the aspirations of free India. In 1947 in his speech he talked of tryst with destiny in which he chartered the path of future India. He was not a religious man but respected the religions values of all religious and advocated a secular state in which all religions had their identity. In politics he was non-aligned, a link between the capitalist West and Marxist East. In his social world-view he was a scientific-humanist respecting science and humanism.

Learned as he was he wrote valuable letters to Indira Gandhi from jail, which are introspective and self-analytical. **Glimpses of India** and **The Discovery of India** are two of his significant books.

In this prose-piece he presents his ideas on the essential unity of India, what he called "unity in diversity". The diversity and varieties one sees are superficial.

The Pathan from the East-West and the Tamil of the South are apparently different, but the great cauldron of Indian civilization which received various races, way of life and religions amalgammated them and gave strength to the essential Indianness. Because of this unique tolerance and acceptance a great wisdom dawned and through the process of synthesis Indian civilization developed unique tenacity and value. Because of this essential unity an Indian Christian, an Indian Moslem, a Sikh, a Parsi, a Buddhist and a Hindu have one identity—Indian.

References

Diversity — variety, varied, different

Feudal — an odd social system in which people received land and protection from the landowners. In the last 150 years in India it mostly stood for exploitation and mis-rule.

Alien — foreign, one who is neither born in the country nor has adopted the citizenship of the country. Presently this idea is beeing subdued as the idea of world citizenship is emerging.

Equater — imaginary line around the earth of an equal distance from the North and South poles.

Heritage — things, ideas and values that have been passed from the earlier generation.

Traits — characteristics

Gurgling — sound like water flowing from a narrow-necked bottle.

❑

ON WITH THE WORK

JAWAHAR LAL NEHRU

On a day like this we should try to detach. ourselves from the problems of the moment and see from a distance, as it were, what is happening in our country and in the world. It is right that we forget our little troubles for a while and think of the major currents that are flowing in our country.

Thirty years ago there appeared on the Indian scene a mighty man of destiny who lighted our path. That light illumined our minds and hearts, and large numbers of our people, forgetting their own troubles and domestic difficulties, their property and family, responded to this call. It was not for personal gain of any kind. Among these there existed a friendly competition as to who could serve the motherland better and more effectively. Our consuming obsession was the liberation of our country. The star of a free India beckoned us forward. We dreamed of freedom from poverty and distress. We gained our political freedom at last but the other freedom still remains for us to achieve.

Unarmed and peaceful, we faced a proud empire, not looking for aid to any other country and relying only on ourselves. We had faith in our leader, our country and in ourselves. This gave us the strength that sustained us during our struggle for independence. If we had faith and self-confidence when to outward seeming we were powerless, then surely we are much better off today when we are a free people with the strength of a great country behind us. Why then should our faith and our confidence in ourselves weaken ? It is true that we have remendous economic and other difficulties to face. But we have faced even bigger problems in the past. Why should we not face these in the same way also ? We must not let our minds get entangled in petty questions and difficulties and forget the main issues.

We belong to a great country, a country that is great not only physically but in things far more important. If we are to be worth of our country, we must have big minds and big hearts, for small men cannot face big issues or accomplish big tasks. Let each one of us do his duty to his country and to his people and not dwell too much on the duty of others. Some people get into the habit of criticizing other without doing anything themselves. Nothing good can come of that type of criticism.

I want you to think for a moment of the days when we fought the battle of India's freedom without arms and without much by way of resources. We had a great leader who inspired us. We had other leaders, too, but it was the masses of this country that bore the brunt of the struggle. They had faith in their country and their leaders and they relied upon themselves. Today, we have more strength then we ever had. It is, therefore, surprising that some people should feel dejected, have no confidence in themselves, and complain all the time.

Let us get back the purposefulness, the enthusiasm, the self-confidence and the faith which moved us at the time of our struggle for freedom. Let us put aside our petty quarrels and factions and think only of the great objective before us.

A nation's work never ends. Men may come and go, generations may pass but the life of a nation goes on. We must remember the basic fact that we can achieve little unless there is peace in the country, no matter what policy we pursue. There are some misguided people who indulge in violence and try to create disorder. I wonder how anybody with the least intelligence can think in terms of such anti-national activities. Therefore, it is the duty of everyone, no matter what his politics, to help in the maintenance of peace in the country.

The people have every right to change the law and even to change governments and they can exercise that right in a peaceful and democratic manner. But those who choose the path of violence have no faith in democracy. If their way were to prevail, there would be complete chaos in the country and the condition of the people would deteriorate even more. All progress would cease and the next few generations would have to carry a heavy burden.

We must learn to depend on ourselves and not look to others for help every time we are in trouble. Certainly we want to make friends with the rest of the world. We also seek the good will and co-operation of all those who reside in this country, whatever their race or nationality. We welcome help and co-operation from every quarter but we muswt depend primarily on our own resources. We should not forget that those who lean too much on others tend to become weak and helpless themselves. A country's freedom can be preserved only by her own strength and self-reliance.

We are not hoptile to any country and we do not want to meddle in other people's affiars. Every nation should be free to choose the path it considers best. We do not wish to interfere with the freedom of other natioins and we do not want them to interfere with our freedom. We are determined to make every possible effort in the cause of peace, for another world was will spell ruin and we shall not escape the general disaster.

Let us, therefore, learn to study our country's problems in the large perspective of the world and let us not permit the minor questions of the day to overwhelm us. I have faith in India and her great destiny. A country must have military strength; but armed power does not by itself constitute a country's real strength. Her real strength lies in the capacity of her people for disciplined work. Only hard work can produce wealth for us and rid us of our poverty.

Each one of us, man or woman, young or old, must therefore, toil and work. Rest is not for us. We did not win freedom so that we might rest afterwards, but in order to work harder to hold and strengthen that freedom. There is a great difference between the voluntary labour of a free man for an objective of his choice and the drudgery of a slave. Our labours as free men and women will lay the foundations for a great future and our love of labour for the cause of India and her people will endure; so will the fact that we are building, brick by brick, the great mansion of a free India. There is joy in such work and, even when we have departed, that work will be there for future generations to see. What is vital and important for us is to keep before us the picture of a great India. India is enduring and will continue to be there long after we are gone.

ON WITH THE WORK

About the Author

This extract is an abridged adaptation of a speech made by Jawaharlal Nehru from the Red Fort on 15th August, 1949. Here he gives a brief outline of the problems facing India and of the foreign policy of the Government and suggests how we can all build the great mansion of a free India. He gave the famous slogan **'Aram Haram Hai'.**

The speech given long back, is still relevant. The speech was first printed in Jawaharlal Nehru's speeches, 1949-53 published by the Publication Division, Ministry of information and Broadcasting, Govt. of India.

❑

ON BEING A BORE

ROBERT LYND

"Don't become a bomb-bore" so the Sunday Express counsels its reader, and it suggests that, though people are interested in their own bombs, they are merely bored by other people's bombs. I confess I am still unsophisticated enough to find my friend's bombs interesting the sometimes even exciting. If I am told of friend's having been bombed out of his house, I feel no desire to change the subject to the abandonment of racing at New-market. Bombs are still too much of a novelty to be dull. Besides, they are higly dangerous. Their explosions are also incidents in what may well be the most importnat battle in the world's history.

There are, I agree, people who can make talk about bombs intensely boring. They are the people who can talk about nothing else - people who seem to find comfort in spreading gruesome stories of destruction, most of them unfounded. Here, I think, however, it is not the subject, but the person that is boring. The bore of war-time is merely the bore of peace-time with a different story to tell. The man who cannot make his bomb interesting, it seems to me, must be a poor narrator.

There are, of course, some people who are bored by almost any conversation. There are bored if you talk shop; they are bored if you talk golf; they are bored if you talk politics. It is men of this kind who complain about talkative barbers and who loathe strangers who try to enter into conversation with them in railway trains. There is a story told of a rich American whom a friend saw one day buying a dollar watch in a great railway station—I think it was at New York. "What are you doing that for ?" said the friend; "haven't you got a watch ?" "I have," said the rich man; "this is for the train bore. Don't you realise that on every train there is a bore and that, almost as soon as you have started on the first day's journey, he comes and sits beside you in the observation car and tries to get into talk with you by asking you what time it is ? Well, I always carry one of these watches with me, and when the train bore comes and sits down beside me and asks me the time I take it out, look at it, and tell him "Half-past two", or whatever time it is and, making faces like a lunatic, fling the watch out of the train. The settles him. Of course he thinks I'm mad and slinks off without waiting to say "Thank you" and tells the other passengers. After that I can travel in peace right across the Continent. I have never known it to fail and it's cheap at the price."

This dislike of conversation with strangers is for me hard to understand. I think I should even enjoy an occasional half-hour with the train bore. Up to a point I like bores. I like overhearing golf bores asking each other whether they know the seventh hole at Wookey and the bunker before the eleventh hole at Stookey. Many bores are so obviously happy that it is a pleasure to watch them. Think of all those motoring bores who not so many years ago, when cars and roads-surfaces were not so good, used to talk for hours of the hills they had been up and down. It was all "Did it in top," "It's one in four isn't it ?" and "It was so steep we had to turn the car and go up it in reverse." Beggar's Roost and Countisbury were god sends to them. You might have imagined from listening to them the they were heroes out of Homer narrating immortal exploits. How boring it would all have been if it had been put down in print. Yet of the motoring bore it might have been said : The greater the bore, the greater the beatitude.

The worst bores, I some times think, are those who love telling people the various routes from one place to another. I have never been more bored in my life than when listening to an old gentleman explaining to an old lady the several ways in which she might have come from Notting Hill Gate to Hampstead. She had complained of the time the journey had taken and immediately he was off on a long rigmarole consisting of the numbers of buses and the names of streets and stations. He went on in a flat voice conducting her as it seemed to me, through every street in west and north London. He told her of all the various places where she might have changed buses and named most of the public-houses on they way. In the end, it seemed to me, he was boring himself as well as the rest of us; but he dared not stop. I fancy, because he could think of nothing else to talk about. By the time he rose to go I was in a coma with words like Camden High Street, Prince of Wales Road and Britannia jostling each other in my brain.

Another boring form of conversation is that of the man who, when talking politics, trots out all the old threadbare arguments with the air of a person using them for the first time. I have been a bore of this kind myself.

As a boy I was blind enough to regard Mr. Gladstone's proposal of Home Rule for Ireland as both dangerous and wicked, and whenever, I met a great friend of mine who was a Home Ruler, I would drag the conversation round to the great theme. I shouted the wildest nonsense into his ear as I walked beside him in the streets, telling him with blazing eyes of all the good England had done to Ireland and yelling all the usual musty quotations from the pre-Home-Rule Gladstone and Sir William Harcourt. Not once did I use an original argument, for I knew none. I was merely an infuriated parrot, speaking out of the richest store of ignorance conceivable. Signs of distress on his patient face could not stop me; but one day, driven beyond endurance, he turned to me with a slight flush and said quietly : "My God, what a bore you are !" Now no one likes to be thought a bore, and it is difficult to go on arguing with a man who tells you that you are boring him. To realise that one is boring somebody is to become a pricked balloon. I certainly did. La Rochefoucauld tells us that. "We can forgive those who bore us, but we cannot forgive those whom we bore," Yet, after the first moment of shock, I never liked my friend the less for his candour. Since then I must have bored many people; but outside the family circle no one has since told me that I was boring them. I have to study the expression on their faces to know.

There are certain people, however, with whom one has a right to be bored - people who are so self-centred that they cannot listen to anyone else talking, people who engage in long conversations with their cats when visitors are present, people who exchange endless reminiscences of their old school when in the company of a man who was at a different school. Such people are boring because they make one feel for the time being an outsider.

When we meet on common ground, however, and indulge in a give-and-take of experiences that we have all shared, there is no excuse for drooping spirits. In the last war the food shortage was a lively if monotonous subject, for we were all victims of it. In the present war air raids are the great theme of talk, and it may be that people endure them all the better for having a friendly ear to which to impart their experiences and thoughts. The talk about them all the time would be insufferable; but five minutes" talk about them now and then is a natural piece of self-indulgence. I would rather talk about Canada or birds or old watches-but if any man has a story to tell of a fairly narrow escape from a falling bomb I will promise neither to think him nor to call him a bore.

ON BEING A BORE

About the Author

Robert Lynd (1879-1949) was a 20th century English essayist and literaryEditor of **New Chronicles.** His essays are humourous and the satirical note enhances their merit. He had a keen sense of language; his choice of words and coinage of words and expressions give his writings uniqueness.

This essay is a reflection on being bored by other people's ideas and preoccupations. In modern times the assertion of one's individuality leads to interest in one's own ideas and thoughts. It also causes a sort of indifference to other's voice. In this insulated modern time one gets easily bored. If there is a give and take attitude then, perhaps, people will not be bored by other's talk and also not bore others by one's own conversation. Lynd humoursly says that people love their own 'bomb' and are scared and bored by other people's bomb. This bomb is nothing but the ideosyncracy of people. He also discusses varieties of talkative bores, train bores, golf bores, politics bore. The worst bore is one whose egoistic assertion makes him feel his birthright and need to enlighten others.

References

Baggar's Roost	— a steep hill road
Banker	— sandy hollow in a golf course.
Contesbury	— a steep hill
God sent	— unexpected yet desirable
Slink	— to move in a stealthy manner or awkwardly.
Homer	— Greek epic poet who wrote **Iliad.**
Musty question	— odd, stale quotations or references.
Rigmarole	— meaninglass talk, complisated procedure, not straight forward i.e., beating about a bush

❑

THE PURLOINED LETTER

EDGAR ALLAN POE

Nil sapientiae odiosius acumine nimio. SENEGA.

At Paris, just after dark one gusty evening in the autumn of 18—, I was enjoying the twofold luxury of meditation and a meerschaum, in company with my friend C. Auguste Dupin, in his little back library, or book-closet, au troisieme, No. 33, Rue Dunot, Faubourg St. Germain. For one hour at least we had maintained a profound silence; while each, to any casual observer, might have seemed intently and exclusively occupied with the curling eddies of smoke that oppressed the atmosphere of the chamber. For myself, however, I was mentally discussing certain topics which had formed matter for conversation between us at an earlier period of the evening; I mean the affair of the Rue Morgue, and the mystery attending the murder of Marie Roget. I looked upon it, therefore, as something of a coincidence, when the door of our apartment was thrown open and admitted our old acquaintance, Monsieur G—, the Prefect of the Parisian police.

We gave him a hearty welcome; for there was nearly half as much of the entertaining as of the contemptible about the man, and we had not seen him for several years. We had been sitting in the dark, and Dupin now arose for the purpose of lighting a lamp, but sat down again, without doing so, upon G—'s saying that he had called to consult us, or rather to ask the opinion of my friend, about some official business which has occasioned a great deal of trouble.

'If it is any point requiring reflection,' observed Dupin, as he forbore to enkindle the wick, 'we shall examine it to better purpose in the dark.'

'That is another of your odd notions,' said the Perfect, who had a fashion of calling everything 'odd' that was beyond his comprehension, and thus lived amid an absolute legion of 'oddities'.

'Very true,' said Dupin, as he supplied his visitor with a pipe, and rolled towards him a comfortable chair.

'And what is the difficulty now?' I asked. 'Nothing more in the assassination way, I hope?'

'Oh no; nothing of that nature. The fact is, the business is very simple indeed, and I make no doubt that we can manage it sufficiently well ourselves; but then I thought Dupin would like to hear the details of it, because it is so excessively odd.'

'Simple and odd,' said Dupin.

'Why, yes; and not exactly that, either. The fact is, we have all been a good deal puzzled because, the affair is so simple and yet baffles us altogether.'

'Perhaps it is the very simplicity of the thing which puts you at fault,' said my friend.

'What nonsense you do talk!' replied the Perfect, laughing heartily.

'Perhaps the mystery is a little too plain,' said Dupin.

'Oh, good heavens! who ever heard of such an idea?'

'A little too self-evident.'

'Ha! ha! ha!—ha! ha! ha!—ho! ho! ho!'—roared our visitor, profoundly amused, 'oh, Dupin, you will be the death of me yet!'

'And what, after all, is the matter on hand?' I asked.

'Why, I will tell you,' replied the Perfect, as he gave a long, steady, and contemplative puff, and settled himself in his chair. 'I will tell you in a few words; but, before I begin, let me caution you that this is an affair demanding the greatest secrecy, and that I should most probably lose the position I now hold, were it known that I confided it to any one.'

'Proceed,' said I.

'Or not,' said Dupin.

'Well, then; I have received personal information, from a very high quarter, that a certain document of the last importance, has been purloined from the royal apartments'.

'The individual who purloined it is known; this beyond a doubt; he was seen to take it. It is known, also, that it still remains in his possession.'

'How is this known?' asked Dupin.

'It is clearly inferred,' replied the Perfect, 'from the nature of the document, and from the non-appearance of certain results which would at once arise from its passing out of the robber's possession;—that is to say, from his employing it as he must design in the end to employ it.'

'Be a little more explicit,' I said.

'Well, I may venture so far as to say that the paper gives its holder a certain power in a certain quarter where such power is immensely valuable.' The Perfect was fond of the cant of diplomacy.

'Still I do not quite understand,' said Dupin.

'No? Well; the disclosure of the document to a third person, who shall be nameless, would bring in question the honour of a personage of most exalted station; and this fact gives the holder of the document an ascendancy over the illustrious personage whose honour and peace are so jeopardized.'

'But this ascendancy,' I interposed, 'would depend upon the robber's knowledge of the loser's knowledge of the robber. Who would dare—'

'The thief,' said G—, 'is the Minister D—, who dares all things, those unbecoming as well as those becoming a man. The method of the theft was not less ingenious than bold. The document in question—a letter, to be frank—had been received by the personage robbed while alone in the royal boudoir. During its perusal she was suddenly interrupted by the entrance of the other exalted personage from whom especially it was her wish to conceal it. After a hurried and vain endeavour to thrust it in a drawer, she was forced to place it, open as it was, upon a table. The address, however, was super most, and, the contents thus unexposed, the letter escaped notice. At this juncture enters the Minister D—. His lynx eye immediately perceives the paper, recognises the handwriting of the address, observes the confusion of the personage addressed, and fathoms her secret. After some business transactions, hurried through in his ordinary manner, he produces a letter somewhat similar to the one in question, opens it, pretends to read it, and then places it in close juxtaposition to the other. Again he converses, for some fifteen minutes, upon the public affairs. At length, in taking leave, he takes also from the table the letter to which he had no claim. Its rightful owner saw, but, of course, dared not call attention to the act, in the presence of the third personage who stood at her elbow. The minister decamped; leaving his own letter—one of no importance—upon the table.'

'Here, then,' said Dupin to me, 'you have precisely what you demand to make the ascendancy complete—the robber's knowledge of the loser's knowledge of the robber.'

'Yes,' replied the Perfect; 'and the power thus attained has, for some months past, been wielded, for political purposes, to a very dangerous extent. The personage robbed is more thoroughly convinced, every day, of the necessity of reclaiming her letter. But this, of course, cannot be done openly. In fine, driven to despair, she has committed the matter to me.'

'Than whom,' said Dupin, amid a perfect whirlwind of smoke, 'no more sagacious agent could, I suppose, be desired, or even imagined.'

'You flatter me,' replied the Perfect; 'but it is possible that some such opinion may have been entertained.'

'It is clear,' said I, 'as you observe, that the letter is still in possession of the minister; since it is this possession, and not any employment of the letter, which bestows the power. With the employment the power departs.'

'True,' said G—; 'and upon this conviction I proceeded. My first care was to make thorough search of the minister's hotel; and here my chief embarrassment lay in the necessity of searching without his knowledge. Beyond all things, I have been warned of the danger which would result from giving him reason to suspect our design.'

'But,' said I, 'you are quite au fait in these investigations. The Parisian police have done this thing often before.'

'Oh yes; and for this reason I did not despair. The habits of the minister gave me, too, a great advantage. He is frequently absent from home all night. His servants are by no means numerous. They sleep at a distance from their master's apartment, and, being chiefly Neapolitans, are readily made drunk. I have keys, as you know, with which I can open any chamber or cabinet in Paris. For three months a night has not passed, during the greater part of which I have not been engaged, personally, in ransacking the D—Hotel. My honor is interested, and, to mention a great sectret; the reward is enormous. So I did not abandon the search until I had become fully satisfied that the thief is a more astute man than myself. I fancy that I have investigated every nook and corner of the premises in which it is possible that the paper can be concealed.'

'But is it not possible,' I suggested, 'that although the letter may be in possession of the minister, as it unquestionably is, he may have concealed it elsewhere than upon his own premises?'

'This is barely possible,' said Dupin. 'The present peculiar condition of affairs at court, and especially of those intrigues in which D—is known to be involved, would render the instant availability of the document—its susceptibility of being produced at a moment's notice—a point of nearly equal importance with its possession.'

'Its susceptibility of being produced,' said I.

'That is to say, of being destroyed,' said Dupin.

'True,' I observed; 'the paper is clearly then upon the premises. As for its being upon the person of the minister, we may consider that as out of the question.'

'Entirely,' said the Perfect. 'He has been twice waylaid, as if by footpads, and his person rigorously searched under my own inspection.'

'You might have spared yourself this trouble,' said Dupin. 'D—, I presume, is not altogether a fool, and, if not, must have anticipated these waylayings, as a matter of course.'

'No altogether a fool,' said G—, 'but then he's a poet, which I take to be only one remove from a fool.'

'True,' said Dupin, after a long and thoughtful whiff from his meerschaum, 'although I have been guilty of certain doggerel myself.'

'Suppose you detail,' said I, 'the particulars of your search.'

'Why the fact is, we took our time, and we searched everywhere. I have had long experience in these affairs. I took the entire building, room by room; devoting the nights of a whole week to each. We examined, first, the furniture of each apartment. We opened every possible drawer; and I presume you know that, to a properly trained police agent, such a thing as a secret drawer is impossible. Any man is a dolt who permits a 'secret' drawer to escape him in a search of this kind. The thing is so plain. There is a certain amount of bulk—of space—to be accounted for in every cabinet. Then we have accurate rules. The fiftieth part of a line could not escape us. After the cabinets we took the chairs. The cushions we probed with the fine long needles you have seen me employ. From the tables we removed the tops.'

'Why so?'

'Sometimes the top of a table, or other similarly arranged piece of furniture, is removed by the person wishing to conceal an article; then the leg is excavated, the article deposited within the cavity, and the top replaced. The bottoms and tops of bed-posts are employed in the same way.'

'But could not the cavity be detected by sounding? I asked.

'By no means, if, when the article is deposited, a sufficient wadding of cotton, be placed around it. Besides, in our case, we were obliged to proceed without noise.'

'But you could not have removed—yo could not have taken to pieces all articles of furniture in which it would have been possible to make a deposit in the manner you mention. A letter may be compressed into a thin spiral roll, not differing much in shape or bulk from a large knitting-needle, and in this form it might be inserted into the rung of a chair, for example. You did not take to pieces all the chairs?'

'Certainly not; but we did better—we examined the rungs of every chair in the hotel, and, indeed, the jointings of every description of furniture, by the aid of a most powerful microscope. Had there been any traces of recent disturbance we should not have failed to detect it instantly. A single grain of gimlet-dust, for example, would have been as obvious as an apple. Any disorder in the glueing—any unusual gaping in the joints—would have sufficed to insure detection.'

'I presume you looked to the mirrors, between the boards and the plates, and you probed the beds and the bed-clothes, as well as the curtains and carpets.'

'That of course; and when we had absolutely completed every particle of the furniture in this way, then we examined the house itself. We divided its entire surface into compartments, which we numbered, so that not one might be missed; then we scrutinised each individual square inch throughout the premises, including the two houses immediately adjoining, with the microscope, as before.'

'The two houses adjoining!' I exclaimed. 'You must have had a great deal of trouble.'

'We had; but the reward offered is prodigious.'

'You include the grounds about the houses?'

'All the grounds are paved with brick. They gave us comparatively little trouble We examined the moss between the bricks, and found it undisturbed.'

'You looked among D—'s papers, of course, and into the books of the library?'

'Certainly; we opened every package and parcel; we not only opened every book, but we turned over every leaf in each volume, not contenting ourselves with a mere shake, according to the fashion of some of our police officers. We also measured the thickness of every book-cover, with the most accurate admeasurement, and applied to each the most jealous scrutiny of the mocroscope. Had any of the bindings been recently meddled with, it would have been utterly impossible that the fact should have escaped observation. Some five or six volumes, just from the hands of the binder, we carefully probed, longitudinally, with the needless.'

'You explored the floors beneath the carpets?'

'Beyond doubt. We removed every carpet, and examined the boards with the microscope.'

'And the paper on the walls?'

'Yes.'

'You looked into the cellars?'

'We did.'

'Then,' I said, 'you have been making a miscalculation, and the letter is not upon the premises, as you suppose.'

'I fear you are right there,' said the Perfect. 'And now, Dupin, what would you advise me to do?'

'To make a through re-search of the premises.'

'That is absolutely needless,' replied G—. 'I am not more sure that I breathe than I am that the letter is not at the Hotel.'

'I have no better advice to give you,' said Dupin. 'You have, of course, an accurate description of the letter?'

'Oh yes!—And here the Perfect, producing a memorandum book, proceeded to read aloud a minute account of the internal, and especially of the external appearance of the missing document.Soon after finishing the perusal of this description, he took his departure, more entirely depressed in spirits than I had ever known the good gentleman before.

In about a month afterwards he paid us another visit, and found us occupied very nearly as before. He took a pipe and a chair and entered into some ordinary conversation. At length I said,—

'Well, but G—, what of the purloined letter? Ipresume you have at last made up your mind that there is no such thing as overreaching the minister?'

'Confound him, say I—yes; I made the re-examination, however, as Dupin suggested—but it was all labor lost, as I knew it would be.'

'How much was the reward offered, did you say?' asked Dupin.

'Why, a very great deal—a very liberal reward—I don't like to say how much, precisely; but one thing I will say, that I wouldn't mind giving my individual check for fifty thousand francs to any one who could obtain me that letter. The fact is, it is becoming of more and more importance every day; and the reward has been lately doubled. If it were trebled, however, I could do no more than I have done.'

'Why, yes,' saidDupin, drawlingly, between the whiffs of his meerschaum, 'I really—think, G—, you have not exerted yourself—to the utmost in this matter. You might—do a little more, I think, eh?'

'How?—in what way?'

'Why—puff, puff—you might—puff, puff—employ cousnel in the matter, eh?—puff, puff. Do you remember the story they tell of Abernethy?'

'No; hang Abernethy!'

'To be sure ! hang him and welcome. But, once upon a time, a certain rich miser conceived the design of sponging upon this Abernethy for a medical opinion. Getting up, for this purpose, an ordinary conversation in a private company, he insinuated his case to the physician as that of an imaginary individual.'

"We will suppose," said the miser, "that his symptoms are such and such; now, doctor, what would you have directed him to take?"

"Take!" said Abernethy, "why, take advice, to be sure."

'But,' said the Prefect, a little dicomposed, 'I am perfectly willing to take advice, and to pay for it. I would really give fifty thousand francs to any one who would aid me in the matter.'

'In that case,' replied Dupin, opening a drawer, and producing a check-book, 'you may as well fill me up a check for the amount mentioned. When you have signed it, I will hand you the letter.'

I was astounded. The Prefect appeared absolutely thunder-stricken. For some minutes he remained speechless and motionless, looking incredulously at my friend with open mouth, and recovering himself in some measure, he seized a pen, and after several pauses and vacant stares, finally filled up and signed a check for fifty thousand francs, and handed it across the table to Dupin. The latter examined it carefully and deposited it in his pocket-book; then, unlocking an escritoire, took thence a letter and gave it to the Prefect. This functionary grasped it in a perfect agony of joy, opened it with a trembling hand, cast a rapid glance at its contents, and then, scrambling and struggling to the door, rushed at length unceremoniously from the room and from the house, without having uttered a syllable since Dupin had requested him to fill up the check.

When he had gone, my friend entered into some explanations.

'The Parisian ploice,' he said, ' are exceedingly able in their way. They are persevering, ingenious, cunning, and thoroughly versed in the knowledge which their duties seem chiefly to demand. Thus, when

G—detailed to us his mode of searching the premises at the Hotel D—I felt entire confidence in his having made a satisfactory investigation—so far as his labors extended.'

'So far as his labors extended?' said I.

'Yes,' said Dupin. 'The measures adopted were not only the best of their kind, but carried out to absolute perfection. Had the letter been deposited within the range of their search, these fellows would, beyond a question, have found it.'

I merely laughed—but he seemed quite serious in all that he said.

'The measures, then,' he continued, 'were good in their kind, and well executed; their defect lay in their being inapplicable to the case, and to the man. A certain set of highly ingenious resources, are, with the Prefect, a sort of Procrustean bed, to which he forcibly adapts his designs. But he perpetually errors by being too deep or too shallow for the matter in hand; and many a schoolboy is a better reasoner than he. I knew one about eight years of age whose success at guessing in the game of 'even and odd' attracted universal admiration. This game is simple, and is played with marbles. One player holds in his hand a number of these toys, and demands of another whether that number is even or odd. If the guess is right, the guesser wins one; if wrong, he loses one. The boy to whom I allude won all the marbles of the school. Of course he had some principle of guessing; and this lay in mere observation and admeasurement of the astuteness of his opponents. For example, an arrant simpleton is his opponent, and, holding up his closed hand, asks, "are they even or odd?" Our schoolboy replies, "odd" and loses; but upon the second trial he wins, for he then says to himself, "the simpleton had them even upon the first trial, and his amount of cunning is just sufficient to make him have them odd upon the second; I will therefore guess "odd"; —he guesses odd, and wins. Now, with a simpleton a degree above the first, he would have reasoned thus :

"This fellow finds that in the first instance I guessed odd, and, in the second, he will propose to himself upon the first impulse, a simple variation from even to odd, as did the first simpleton; but then a second thought will suggest that this is too simple a variation, and finally he will decide upon putting it even as before. I will therefore guess even",—he guesses even, and wins. Now this mode of reasoning in the schoolboy, whom his fellows termed "lucky",—what, in its last analysis, is it?'

'It is merely,' I said, 'an identification of the reasoner's intellect with that of his opponent.'

'It is,' said Dupin; 'and, upon inquiring of the boy by what means he effected the thorough identification in which his success consisted, I received answer as follows: "When I wish to find out how wise, or how stupid, or how good, or how wicked is any one, or what are his thoughts at the moment, I fashion the expression of my face, as accurately as possible, in accordance with the expression of his, and then wait to see what thoughts or sentiments arise in my mind or heart, as if to match or correspond with the expression." This response of the schoolboy lies at the bottom of all the spurious profundity which has been attributed to Rochefoucauld, to La Bougive, to Machiaveli, and to Campanella.'

'And the identificaiton' I said, 'of the reasoner's intellect with that of his opponent, depends, if I understand you aright, upon the accuracy with which the opponent's intellect is admeasured.'

'For its practical value it depends upon this,' replied Dupin; and the Prefect and his cohort fail so frequently, first, by default of this identification, and, secondly, by ill-admeasurement, or rather through non-admeasurement, of the intellect with which they are engaged. They consider only their own ideas of ingenuity; and, in searching for anything hidden, advert only to the modes in which they would have hidden it. They are right in this much—that their own ingenuity is a faithful representative of that of the mass; but when the cunning of the individual felon is diverse in character from their own, the felon foils them, of course. This always happens when it is above their own, and very usually when it is below. They have no variation of principle in their investigations; at best, when urged by some unusual emergency—by some extraordinary reward—they extend or exaggerate their old modes of practice, without touching their principles. What, for example, in this case of D—has been done to vary the principle of action? What is all this boring, and probing, and sounding, and scrutinising with the microscope, and dividing the surface of the building into registered square inches—what is it all but an exaggeration of the application of the one principle or set of principles of search, which are based upon the one set of notions regarding human ingenuity, to which the Prefect, in the long routine of his duty, has been accustomed? Do you not see he has taken it for granted that all men proceed to conceal a letter,— not exactly in a gimlet-hole bored in a chair-leg—but, at least, in some out-of-the-way hole or corner suggested by the same tenor of thought which would urge a man to secrete a letter in a gimlet-hole bored in a chair-leg? And do you not see also, that such recherche nooks for concealment are adopted only for ordinary occasions, and would be adopted only by ordinary intellects; for, in all cases of concealment, a disposal of the article concealed—a disposal of it in this recherche manner,— is, in the very first instance, presumable and presumed; and thus its discovery depends, not at all upon the acumen, but altogether upon the mere care, patience, and determination of the seekers; and where the case is of importance—or, what amounts to the same thing in the policial eyes, when the reward is of magnitude,—the qualities in question have never been known to fail. You will now understand what I meant in suggesting that had the purloined letter been hidden anywhere within the limits of the Prefect's examination—in other words, had the principle of its concealment been comprehended within the principles of the Prefect—its discovery would have been a matter altogether beyond question. This functionary, however, has been thoroughly mystified; and the remote source of his defeat lies in the supposition that the minister is a fool, because he has acquired renown as a poet. All fools are poets; this the Prefect feels; and he is merely guilty of a non distributio medi in thence inferring that all poets are fools.'

'But is this really the poet?' I asked. 'There are two brothers, I know; and both have attained reputation in letters. The minister, I believe, has written learnedly on the Differential Calculus. He is a mathematician, and no poet.'

You are mistaken; I know him well; he is both. As poet and mathematician, he would reason well; as mere mathematician, he could not have reasoned at all, and thus would have been at the mercy of the Prefect.'

'You surprise me,' I said, 'by these opinions, which have been contradicted by the voice of the world. You do not mean to set at naught the well-digested idea of centuries. The mathematical reason has long been regarded as the reason par excellence.'

"Il a aparier," 'replied Dupin, quoting from Chamfort, "que taute idee publique, toute convention recue, est une sottise, car elle a convenu au plus grand nombre." The mathematicians, I grant you, have done their best to promulgate the popular error to which you allude, and which is none the less an error for its promulgation as truth. With an art worthy a better cause, for example they have insinuated the term 'analysis' into application to algebra. The French are the originators of the particular deception; but if a term is of any importance—if words derive any value from applicability—then "analysis" conveys "algebra" about as much as, in Latin, "ambitus" implies "ambition", "religio", "religion," or "honines honesti," "a set of honourable men."

'You have a quarrel on hand, I see,' said I, 'with some of the algebraists of Paris; but proceed.'

'I dispute the availability, and thus the value, of that reason which is cultivated in any especial form other than the abstractly logical. I dispute, in particular, the reason, educed by mathematical study. The mathematics are the science of form and quantity; mathematical reasoning is merely logic applied to observation upon form and quantity. The great error lies in supposing that even the truths of what is called pure algebra, are abstract or general truths. And this error is so egregious that I am confounded at the universality with which it has been received. Mathematical axioms are not axioms of general truth. What is true of relation—of form and quantity— is often grossly false in regard to morals, for example. In this latter science it is very usually untrue that the aggregated parts are equal to the whole. In chemistry also the axiom fails. In the consideration of motive it fails; for two motives, each ofa given value, have not, necessarily, a value when united, equal to the sum of their values apart. There are numerous other mathematical truths which are only truths within the limits of relation. But the mathematician argues, from his finite truths, through habits, as if they were of an absolutely general applicability—as the world indeed imagines them to be. Bryant, in his very learned Mythology, mentions as analogous source of error, when he says that "although the Pagan fables are not believed, yet we forget ourselves continually, and make inferences from them as existing realities." With the algebraists, however, who are Pagans themselves, the "Pagan fables" are believed, and the inferences are made, not so much through lapse of memory, as through an unaccountable addling of the brains. In short, I never yet encountered the mere mathematician who could be trusted out of equal roots, or one who did not clandestinely hold it as a point of his faith that $x^2 + px$ was absolutely and unconditionally equal to q. Say to one of these gentlemen, by way ofexperiment, if you please, that you believe occasions may occur where $x^2 + px$ is not altogether equal to q, and, having made him understand what you mean, get out of his reach as speedily as convenient, for, beyond doubt, he will endeavour to knock you down.'

'I mean to say,' continued Dupin, while I merely laughed at his last observations, 'that if the minister had been no more than a mathematician, the Prefect would have been under no necessity of giving me this check. I knew him, however, as both mathematician and poet, and my measures were adapted to his capacity, with reference to the circumstances by which he was surrounded. I knew him as a courtier, too, and as a bold intrigant. Such a man, I considered, could not fail to be aware of the ordinary policial modes of action. He could not have failed to anticipate—and events have proved that he did not fail to anticipate—the waylayings to which he was subjected. He must have foreseen, I reflected, the secret investigations of his premises. His frequent absences from home at night, which were hailed by the Prefect as certain aids to his success, I regarded only as ruses, to afford opportunity for thorough search to the police, and thus the sooner to impress them with the conviction to which G—, in fact, did finally arrive—the conviction that the letter was not upon the premises. I felt, also, that the whole train of thought, which I was at some pains in detailing to you just now, concerning the invariable principle of policial action in searches for articles concealed—I felt that this whole train of thought would necessarily pass through the mind of the minister. It would imperatively lead him to despise all the ordinary nooks of concealment. He could not, I reflected, be so weak as not to see that the most intricate and remote recess of his hotel would be as open as his commonest closets to the eyes, to the probes, to the gimlets, and to the microscopes of the Prefect. I saw, in fine, that he would be driven, as a matter of course, to simplicity, if not deliberately induced to it as a matter of choice. You will remember, perhaps, how deperately the Prefect laughed when I suggested, upon our first interview, that it was just possible this mystery troubled him so much on account of its being so very self-evident.'

'Yes,' said I, 'I remember his merriment well. I really thought he would have fallen into convulsions.'

'The material world,' continued Dupin, 'abounds with very strict analogies to the immaterial; and thus some colour of truth has been given to the thetorical dogma, that metaphor, or simile, may be made to strengthen an argument, as well as to embellish a description. The principle of the vis inertiae, for example, seems to be identical in physics and metaphysics, It is not more true in the former, that a large body is with more difficulty set in motion than a smaller one, and that its subsequent momentum is commensurate with this difficulty, than it is, in the latter, that intellects of the vaster capacity, while more forcible, more constant, and more eventful in their movements than those of inferior grade, are yet the less readily moved, and more embarrassed and full of hesitation in the first few steps of their progress. Again: have you ever noticed which of the street signs, over the shop doors, are the most attractive of attention?'

'I have never given the matter a thought,' I said.

'There is a game of puzzles,' he resumed, 'which is played upon a map. One party playing requires another to find a given word—the name of town, river, state or empire—any word, in short, upon the motley and perplexed surface of the chart. A novice in the game generally seeks to embarrass his opponents by giving them the most minutely-lettered names; but the adept selects such words as stretch, in large characters, from one end of the chart to the other. These, like the over-largely lettered signs and placards of the street, escape observation by dint of being excessively obvious; and here the physical oversight is precisely analogous with the moral inapprehension by which the intellect suffers to pass unnoticed those considerations which are too obtrusively and too palpably self-evident. But this is a point, it appears, somewhat above or beneath the understanding of the Prefect. He never once thought it probable, or possible, that the minister had deposited the letter immediately beneath the nose of the whole world, by way of best preventing any portion of that world from perceiving it.'

'But the more I reflected upon the daring, dashing and discriminating ingenuity of D—; upon the fact that the document must always have been at hand, if he intended to use it to good purpose; and upon the decisive evidence, obtained by the Prefect, that it was not hidden within the limits of that dignitary's ordinary search—the more satisfied I became that, to conceal this letter, the minister had resorted to the comprehensive and sagacious expedient of not attempting to conceal it at all.

'Full of these ideas, I prepared myself with a pair of green spectacles, and called one fine morning, quite by accident, at the ministerial hotel. I found D—at home, yawning, lounging, and dawdling, as usual, and pretending to be in the last extremity of ennui. He is, perhaps, the most really energetic human being now alive—but that is only when nobody sees him.

'To be even with him, I complained of my weak eyes, and lamented the necessity of the spectacles, under cover of which I cautiously and thoroughly surveyed the apartment, while seemingly intent only upon the conversation of my host.

'I paid special attention to a large writing-table near which he sat, and upon which lay confusedly, some miscellaneous letters and other papers, with one or two musical instruments and a few books. Here, however, after a long and very deliberate scrutiny, I saw nothing to excite particular suspicion.

'At length my eyes, in going the circuit of the room, fell upon a trumpery filigree card-rack of paste-board, that hung dangling by a dirty blue ribbon, from a little brass knob just beneath the middle of the mantel-piece. In this rack, which had three or four compartments, were five or six visiting cards and a solitary letter. This last was much soiled and crumpled. It was torn nearly in two, across the middle—as if a design, in the first instance, to tear it entirely up as worthless, had been altered, or stayed, in the second. It had a large black seal, bearing the D—cipher very conspicuously, and was addressed, in a diminutive female hand, to D—, the minister, himself. It was thrust carelessly, and even, as it seemed, contemptuously, into one of the upper divisions of the rack.

'No sooner had I glanced at this letter, than I concluded it to be that of which I was in search. To be sure, it was, to all appearance, radically different from the one of which the Prefect had read us so minute a description. Here the seal was large and black, with the D—cipher; there it was small and red, with the ducal arms of the S—family. Here, the address, to the minister, was diminutive and feminine; there the superscription, to a certain royal personage, was markedly bold and decided; the size alone formed a point of correspondence. But, then, the radicalness of these differences, which was excessive; the dirt; the soiled and torn condition of the paper, so inconsistent with the true methodical habits of D—, and so suggestive of a design to delude the beholder into an idea of the worthlessness of the document; these things, together with the hyperobtrusive situation of this document, full in the view of every visitor, and thus exactly in accordance with the conclusions to which I had previously arrived; these things, I say, were strongly corroborative of suspicion, in one who came with the intention to suspect.

'I protracted my visit as long as possible, and, while I maintained a most animated discussion with the minister, on a topic which I knew will had never failed to interest and excite him, I keptmy attention really riveted upon the letter. In this examination, I committed to memory its external appearance and arrangement in the rack; and also fell, at length, upon a discovery which set at rest whatever trivial doubt I might have entertained. In scrutinising the edges of the paper, I observed them to be more chafed than seemed necessary. They presented the broken appearance which is manifested when a stiff paper, having been folded and pressed with a folder, is refolded in a reversed direction, in the same creases or edges which had formed the original fold. This discovery was sufficient. It was clear to me that the letter had been turned, as a glove, inside out, redirected, and resealed. I bade the minister good morning, and took my departure at once, leaving a gold snuff-box upon the table.

'The next morning I called for the snuff-box, when we resumed, quite eagerly, the conversation of the preceding day. While thus engaged, however, a loud reports, as if of a pistol, was heard immediately beneath the windows of the hotel, and was succeded by a series of fearful screams, and the shoutings of a mob. D—rushed to a casement, threw it open, and looked out. In the meantime, I stepped to the card-rack, took the letter, put it in my pocket, and replaced it by a facsimile (so far as regards externals), which I had carefully prepared at my lodgings; imitating the D—cipher, very readily, by means of a seal formed of bread.

'The disturbance in the street had been occasioned by the frantie behaviour of a man with a musket. He had fired it among a crowd of women and children. It proved, however, to have been without ball, and the fellow was suffered to go his way as a lunatic or a drunkard. When he had gone, D—came from the window, whither I had followed him immediately upon securing the object in view. Soon afterwards I bade him farewell. The pretended lunatic was a man in my own pay.'

'But what purpose had you,' I asked, 'in replacing the letter by a facsimile? Would it not have been better, at the first visit, to have seized it openly, and departed?'

'D—,' replied Dupin, 'is a desperate man, and a man of nerve. His hotel, too, is not without attendants devoted to his interests. Had I made the wild attempt you suggest, I might never have left the ministerial presence alive. The good people of Paris might have heard of me no more. But I had an object apart from these considerations. You know my political prepossessions. In this matter, I act as a partisan of the lady concerned. For eighteen months the minister has had her in his power. She has now him in hers; since, being unaware that the letter is not in his possession, he will proceed with his exactions as if it was. Thus will he inevitably commit himself, at once, to his political destruction. His downfall, too, will not be more precipitate than awkward. It is all very well to talk about the facilis descensus Averni: but in all kinds of climbing, as Catalani said of singing, it is far more easy to get up than to come down. In the present instance I have no sympathy—at least no pity—for him who descends. He is that monstrum horrendum, an unprincipled man of genius. I confess, however, that I should like very well to know the precise character of his thoughts, when being defied by her whom the Prefect terms "a certain personage", he is reduced to opening the letter which I left for him in the card-rack.'

'How? did you put anything particular in it?'

'Why—it did not seem altogether right to leave the interior blank—that would have been insulting. D—, at Vienna once, did me an evil turn, which I told him, quite good-humouredly, that I should remember. So, as I knew he would feel some curiosity in regard to the identity of the person who had outwitted him, I thought it a pity not to give him a clue. He is well acquainted with my MS., and I just copied into the middle of the blank sheet the words—

'—Un dessein si funeste, S'iln'est digned' Atree, est dignede Thyeste.'

They are to be found in Crebillon's Atree'.

THE PURLOINED LETTER

About the Author

Edgar Allan Poe (1809–1849) was the son of actors, and was born at Boston in United States of America. He went to University of Virginia and later become a journalist, finally moving to become an editor. His achievements as a writer of tales are significant to the art of story writing. The sense of horror and surprise is unique to his tales. His play with the idea of death makes his stories wonderful and special.

"The Purloined letter" reflects a brilliant mind at work. It is written in the detective story pattern. It reminds one of Sherlock Holmes. In it Dupin masterfully succeeds in restoring the stolen letter to its owner. At first glance, the story line appears simple, but it is full of adventure. It shows Poe's skill in story writing and moving logically to achieve the goal.

References

Nil sapien tae...nimes Latin — nothing is more detestable to wisdom than too much subtlety.

Meerschaum — a Tobacco pipe with the bowl made of silicate clay.

Purloined	— stolen
Boudoir	— lady's bedroom, a private sitting room.
Lynx	— quick like a cat
Astute	— shrewd, keen
An fait	— practised.
Nea Politans	— from Naples, Italian
Footpads	— thieves
Doggerel	— comic or burlesque, a rude and crude verse.
Gimlet	— a small boring pointed tool
Glueing	— a strong glue or adhesive made of animal bones.
Escritorie	— a writing table
Procrustean	— like Proscrustus a famous ancient Greek robber, who made his victims conform to the length of his bed by either stretching them or cutting them short.
Cohort	— the police party of the prefect
Felon	— criminal
Spurious profersity	— doubtful wisdom
Rochefoucauld	— 17th Century French novelist
Machiavelli	— 16th century Italian statesman who belived that the state was supreme.
Campanella	— 16th – 17th century Italian philosopher and poet.
Recherche	— (French) uncommon, rare
Acumen	— quickness of perception ability to see and know things quickly.
Non distributio medii	— latin. A middle term which links the premise and couclusion in a logical statement.
Chamfort	— 18th Century French author and novelist.
It a parier...grand nombre	— French. All conventions are a stupidity for they are aimed at masses.

Ambitus, seligio, honesti	— Latin convassing, a sense of rightness, distinguisned.
Egregious	— remarkable in some bad way, glancing, flagrant.
Analogous	— like, comparable
Axiom	— rule, preposition.
Intrigent	— French. one who intrigues or plots schemer.
Ruses	— tricks
Vis inertiae	— Latin. Inherent resistance in a body to charge its state.
Dawding	— spending tense in a trifling manner, a waster.
Ennui	— French boredom
Trumpery	— worthless
Filigree	— ornamental work.
Hyperobtrusive	— over obvious
Prepossessions	— Learnings, views
Facilus discensus Averni	— Latin. indescent to Avernue is easy (Virgil)
Catalani	— 19th Century famous Italian singer.
Monstrum harrendum	— Latin. dreadful creature. .
Un designin ... de Thyerte	— 'A design so deadly. If not worthy of Atreus, is worthy of Thyestes.

❑

THE COUNTRY OF THE BLIND

H. G. WELLS

I

In a remote part of South America there lies that mysterious mountain valley, cut off from the world of men, the Country of the Blind. Long years ago it was possible for men to journey through frightful gorges and over an icy pass into its pleasant meadows. A few people did indeed go, a family or so of Peruvians fleeing from the tyranny of an evil ruler. Then came the earthquake, when there were landslips and sudden floods. One whole side of an old mountain slipped and came down in thunder, and cut off the Country of the Blind for ever from the exploring feet of men.

The valley had in it all that one could desire—sweet water, grassy meadows, a good climate, and slopes of rich brown soil with tangles of a shrub that bore excellent fruit. The settlers did well indeed there. Their animals did well and multiplied, and but one thing marred their happiness. Yes, it was enought to ma it greatly. A strange disease had come upon them, and had made all the children born to them there—blind.

As they grew up, the sightless youngsters were guided hither and thither until they knew the whole valley marvellously well, and when at last the older people died, the race lived on. They had even time to adapt themselves to the blind control of fire, which they made carefully in stoves of stone.

Generation followed generation. They forgot many things; they devised many things. In all things except sight they were strong and healthy. The little community grew in numbers and in understanding, and met and settled social and economic problems that arose. Generation followed generation. Generation followed generation. Then there came a time when a man came by chance into this community from the outer world. And this is the story of that man.

He was a mountaineer. His name was Nunez. He was one of a party working their difficult and almost vertical way up one of the highest mountains in the district. They built a night shelter amidst the snow upon a little shelf of rock, and, presently, they found Nunez had gone from them. They shouted, and there was no reply. They shouted and whistled, and for the rest of that night they slept no more.

When the morning came they saw the marks of his fall. He had slipped eastward towards the unknown side of the mountain. Far below he had struck a steep slope of snow, and down it fell in the midst of a snow avalanche. Far, far below, in the distance, they could see trees rising out of a narrow, shut-in valley—the lost Country of the Blind. But they did not know it was the lost Country of the Blind, nor could they distinguish it in any way from any of the other upland valleys. Frightened by the disaster, they abandoned their search in the afternoon, and returned down the western side of the mountain to their base.

The man who fell survived.

At the end of the slope he fell a thousand feet, and came down in the midst of a cloud of snow upon a snow slope even steeper than the one above. Down this he was whirled, stunned and insensible, but without a bone broken in his body; and then at last came to gentler slopes, and rolled out and lay still in the deep snow. He rested flat upon his chest for a while, wondering where he was and what had happened to him. He felt his limbs, and discovered that several of his buttons were gone and that his coat was turned over his head. His knife had gone from his pocket, and his hat was lost, though he had tied it under his chin. He remembered that he had been looking for loose stones to raise his piece of the shelter wall. His ice-axe had disappeared.

He struggled to his feet, aching in every limb, and got down painfully from the heaped loose snow around his. He went downward to where the snow thinned and eventually disappeared, and there dropped beside a large rock, and immediately fell asleep...

He was awakened by the singing of birds in the trees far below. He sat up and saw that he was at the foot of a vast precipice. Below him it seemed there was a precipice equally steep, but he found a sort of chimney-way dripping with snow-water down which a desperate man might climb. He found it easier than it seemed, and came at last into the valley and the sunlight. He was stiff and weary. He sat down in the shadow of a rock, and remained for a time resting before he went on to the houses.

They were very strange to his eyes, and indeed the whole aspect of that valley became, as he looked at it, queerer and more unfamiliar. The greater part of its surface was soft green meadow, starred with many beautiful flowers, irrigated with extraordinary care. On the higher slopes above this flocks of llamas pulled at the sweet grass. Sheds, apparently shelters or feeding-places for the llamas, stood against the boundary wall here and there. A number of paths paved with black and white stones, and each with a curious little kerb at the side, ran hither and thither in an orderly manner. The houses of the village stood in a continuous row on either side of a street of astonishing cleanness. Here and there was a door, but there were no windows. The walls were coloured with extraordinary irregularity; smeared with a sort of plaster that was sometimes grey, sometimes brick-coloured or dark brown. It was the sight of this wild plastering that first brought the word 'blind' into the thoughts of the explorer. 'The good man who did that,' he thought, 'must have been as blind as a bat.'

He descended a steep place, and so came to a wall that ran round the valley. He could see a number of men and women resting on piled heaps of grass in a part of the meadow, and nearer the village a number of children lying asleep. Nearer to him three men carried pails along a little path that ran from the encircling wall towards the houses. They were dressed in garments of llama cloth and boots and belts of leather. They followed one another in single file, walking slowly and yawning as they walked, like men who have been up all night. After a moment's hesitation Nunez went forward, and gave a loud shout that echoed round the valley.

The three men stopped, and moved their heads as though they were looking around them. But they did not appear to see him, and after a time Nunez shouted again, and then once more, and again the word 'blind' came up to the top of his thoughts. 'The fools must be blind,' he said.

The three stood side by side, not looking at him, but with their ears directed towards him, judging him by his unfamiliar steps. They stood close together like men a little afraid, and he could see their eyelids closed and sunken, as though the eyes beneath had shrunk away. There was an expression of wonder on their faces.

'A man,' one said, '—a man or a spirit—coming down from the rocks.'

But Nunez advanced with the confident steps of a youth who enters upon life. All the old stories of the lost valley and the Country of the Blind were coming back to his mind, and through his thoughts ran this old proverb,

'In the Country of the Blind, the One-eyed Man is King.'

And very politely he greeted them. He talked to them, and used his eyes.

II

'Over the mountains I come,' said Nunez, 'out of the country beyond there—where men can see.'

'See?' muttered one, 'See?'

'He comes,' said the second blind man, 'out of the rocks.

They frightened him by a simultaneous movement towards him, each with a hand outstretched. He stepped back from the advance of these spread fingers.

'Come hither,' said the third blind man, following his motion and clutching him neatly.

And they held Nunez and felt him over, saying no word further until they had done so.

'Carefully,' he cried, with a finger in his eye, and found they thought it, with its fluttering lids, a queer thing in him.

They went over it again.

'Let us lead him to the elders,' said one.

'Shout first,' said the second, 'lest the children be afraid. This is a marvellous occasion.'

So they shouted, and took Nunez by the hand to lead him to the houses.

He drew his hand away. 'I can see,' he said; but turning, stumbled against one of the pails.

'His senses are imperfect,' said the third blind man.

'He stumbles, and talks unmeaning words. Lead him by the hand.'

'As you like,' said Nunez, and was led along, laughing.

It seemed they knew nothing of sight.

Well, in good time he would teach them.

The place seemed larger as he drew near to it, and the smeared plasterings queerer. A crowd of children and men and women came around him, holding on to him, touching him with soft sensitive hands, smelling at him, and listening at every word he spoke. The women and girls, he was pleased to see, had quite sweet faces, even though their eyes were shut and sunken. His three guides kept close to him, and said again and again, 'A wild man out of the rocks.'

'Bring him to the elders.'

And they pushed him suddenly through a doorway into a room as black as ink, except at the end there faintly glowed a fire. The crowd closed in behind him and shut out all but the faintest glimmer of day, and before he could stop himself he had fallen headlong over the feet of a seated man. His arm, out-flung, struck the face of someone else as he went down. He heard a cry of anger, and for a moment he struggled against a number of hands that clutched him.

'I fell down,' he said; 'I couldn't see in this inky darkness.'

There was a pause as if the unseen persons about him tried to understand his words. Then a voice said: 'He is but newly formed. He stumbles as he walks and mixes words that mean nothing with his speech.'

'May I sit up?' he asked, in a pause. 'I will not struggle against you again.'

They consulted, and let him rise.

The voice of an older man began to question him. Nunez found himself trying to explain the great world out of which he had fallen, the sky and mountains and sight and such-like marvels, to these elders who sat in darkness in the Country of the Blind. And they believed and understood nothing of what he told them. They could not even understand many of his words. For fourteen generations these people had been blind and cut off from all the seeing world. The names for all the things of sight had faded and changed; the story of the outer world was a child's story.

Slowly Nunez realized this; and after his poor attempt to explain sight to them had been set aside, he sat listening to their instruction. And the eldest of the blind men explained to him life and philosophy and religion. He explained how the world (meaning their valley) had been first an empty hollow in the rocks, and then had come llamas and a few other creatures that had little sense, and then men, and at last angels, whom one could hear singing and making fluttering sounds, but whom no one could touch at all. This puzzled Nunez greatly until he thought of the birds.

He went on to tell Nunez how time was divided into the warm and the cold, which are the blind equivalents of day and night. How it was good to sleep in the warm and work during the cold, so that now, but for his coming, the whole village of the blind would have been asleep. He said the night—for the blind call their day night—was now far gone, and everyone should go back to sleep. He asked Nunez if he knew how to sleep. Nunez said he did, but that before sleep he wanted food.

They brought him food—llama's milk in a bowl, and rough salted bread— and led him into a lonely place to eat and then to sleep. But Nunez slept not at all.

Instead, he sat up in the place where they had left him, resting his limbs and making plans.

Every now and then he laughed, sometimes with amusement, and sometimes with anger.

'Explaining things as though I were a child!' he said. 'Thinking I've got no senses! They little know they've been insulting their heaven-sent king and master. I see I must teach them a thing or two. Let me think—let me think.'

He was still thinking when the sun set.

III

He heard a voice calling to him from the village.

'Ya ho there! Come hither!'

He stood up smiling. He would show these people once and for all how useful sight was. They would seek him, but not find him.

'You move not,' said the voice.

He laughed noiselessly, and stepped quietly from the path.

'Tread not on the grass; that is not allowed.'

Nunez had scarcely heard the sound he made himself. He stopped amazed.

The owner of the voice came running up the path towards him.

He stepped back into the pathway. 'Here I am,' he said.

'Why did you not come when I called you?' said the blind man. 'Must you be led like a child? Can you not hear the path. as you walk?'

Nunez laughed. 'I can see it,' he said.

'There is no such word as see,' said the blind man, after a pause. 'Stop being foolish, and follow the sound of my feet.'

Nunez followed, a little annoyed.

'My time will come,' he said.

'You'll learn,' the blind man answered. 'There is much to learn in the world.'

'Has no one told you, "In the Country of the Blind, the One-eyed Man is King"?'

'What is blind?' asked the blind man carelessly over his shoulder.

Four days passed, and the fifth found the King of the Blind still a clumsy and useless stranger among his subjects. He found working and going about at night particularly tiresome, and he decided that that should be the first thing he would change.

It was marvellous with what confidence these people moved about. Everything, you see, had been made to fit their needs. Each of the radiating paths of the valley area had a constant angle to the others, and was distinguished by a special notch upon its kerb. All obstacles and irregularities of path or meadow had long since been cleared away. Their senses had become marvellously acute. They could hear and judge the slightest gesture of a man a dozen paces away—could hear the very beating of his heart. Their sense of smell was extraordinarily fine; they could distinguish individual differences as easily as a dog can. And it was only when at last Nunez tried to assert himself that he found how easy and confident their movements could be.

He rebelled only after he had tried persuasion.

He tried at first on several occasions to tell them about sight. He spoke of the beauties of sight, of watching the mountains, of the sky and the sunrise. They told him there were indeed no mountains at all, but that the end of the rocks where the llamas grazed was the end of the world. They said his thoughts were wicked—for they believed that the roofs of caves, which were smooth to touch, were the roof of the world. He saw that he shocked them, and gave up that aspect of the matter altogether, and tried to show them the practical value of sight. One morning he persuaded them to let him go a long way up the sloping meadows towards the wall with one of their old men, and to him he promised to describe all that happened among the houses. He noted certain goings and comings. but of the things that happened inside or behind the windowless houses—the only things they took note of to test him by—he could see or tell nothing.

It was after the failure of this attempt, and when they laughed at him, that he turned to force. In fury he seized a spade, and then he discovered a new thing about himself, that it was impossible for him to hit a blind man.

He hesitated, and found them all aware that he had snatched up the spade. They stood alert, with their heads on one side, and bent their ears towards him for what he would do next.

'Put that spade down,' said one, and he felt a sort of helpless horror.

He pushed one backwards against a house wall, and fled past him and out of the village.

He went across one of their meadows, leaving a track of trampled grass behind his feet, and presently sat down by the side of one of their ways. Far away he saw a number of men carrying spades and sticks come out of the street of houses, and advance in a spreading line along the several paths towards him. They came slowly, speaking frequently to one another, and often the whole cordon would halt and sniff the air and listen.

The first time they did this Nunez laughed. But afterwards he did not laugh.

One found his trail in the trampled grass, and came stooping and feeling his way along it.

For five minutes he watched the slow advance of the cordon, and then he became frightened. He stood up, went a step or so towards the boundary wall, turned, and went back a little way. There they all stood in a crescent, still and listening.

He also stood still, gripping his spade very tightly in both hands. Should he attack them?

He moved along the meadow towards a little door-way in the boundary wall, and directly he moved they followed him. 'I'll kill them if they touch me,' he swore, 'by Heaven, I will. I'll hit.' He called aloud, 'Look here, I'm going to do what I like in this valley. Do you hear? I'm going to do what I like and go where I like!'

They were moving in upon him quickly, groping, yet moving rapidly. It was like playing blind man's buff, with everyone blind folded except one. 'Get hold of him!' cried one. He found himself in the centre of a loose curve of pursuers.

'I'll hurt you', he shouted, sobbing with emotion. By Heaven, I'll hurt you Leave me along!'

He began to run, not knowing clearly where to run. He ran from the nearest blind man, because it would be horrible to hit him. He made for where a gap in the cordon was wide, and the men on either side, hearing him come, rushed in. He sprang forward. and then saw he must be caught, and *swish*! the spade had struck. He felt the soft thud of hand and arm, and the man fell down with a cry of pain, and he was through.

Through! And then he was close to the street of houses again, and more blind men, whirling spades and sticks.

He heard steps behind him just in time, and found a tall man rushing forward and swiping at the sound of him. He lost his nerve, threw his spade but missed, and whirled about and fled, shouting as he dodged another.

He was panic-stricken. He ran wildly to and fro. Far away in the boundary wall he saw the little doorway, and he set off in a wild rush for it. He did not even look round at his pursuers until he had reached and was through it. He climbed a little way among the rocks, and lay down sobbing for breath.

And so his little rebellion came to an end.

He stayed outside the wall of the valley of the Blind for two nights and days without food or shelter. He thought of ways of fighting and conquering these people, and it grew clear that for him no practicable way was possible. He had no weapons, and now it would be hard to get one.

He tried to find food, to catch a llama in order to try to kill it—perhaps by hammering it with a stone. But the llamas looked at him with distrustful brown eyes, and spat when he drew near. Fear came on him the second day and fits of shivering.

Finally he crawled down to the wall, shouting, until two blind men came out of the gate and talked to him.

'I was mad,' he said. 'But I was only newly made.'

They said that was better.

He told them he was wiser now, and was sorry for all he had done.

Then he wept, for he was very weak and ill, and they took that as a favourable sign.

They asked him if he still thought he could 'see.'

'No,' he said. 'That was foolish. The word means nothing—less than nothing!'

They asked him what was overhead.

'About ten times the height of a man there is a roof above the world—of rock—and very, very smooth.'

He burst again into wild tears. 'Before you ask me any more, give me some food or I shall die.'

He expected punishment, but these blind people were tolerant. They regarded his rebellion as proof of his idiocy and inferiority. They gave him the simplest and heaviest work, and he, seeing no other way of living, did what he was told.

IV

So Nunez became a citizen of the Country of the Blind, and came to know some of its people well. There was Yacob, his master, a kind man when not annoyed; and there was Medina, who was the youngest daughter of Yacob. Nunez thought her beautiful. Her closed eyelids lay as though they might open again at any moment. There was a tenderness in her face, and her hair shone like silver in the moonlight.

He talked to her whenever he could take an opportunity. Very timidly he spoke to her of sight. She listened to his description of the stars and the mountains and her own sweet beauty. She did not believe, she could only half understand, but she was mysteriously delighted, and it seemed to him that she completely understood.

It was one of her elder sisters who first told Yacob that Medina and Nunez were in love.

There was from the first very great opposition to the marriage of Nunez and Medina because he was thought to be not as intelligent as the blind people of the valley. Her sisters opposed it bitterly as bringing discredit on them all. Old Yacob, though he had formed a sort of liking for his clumsy obedient servant, shook his head and said that marriage was impossible.

'You see, my dear,' he said to his daughter, 'he's and diot. He can't do anything right.'

'I know,' wept Medina. 'But he's better than he was. He's getting better. And he's strong, dear father, and kind—stronger and kinder than any otherman in the world. And he loves me—and, father, I love him'.

Old Yacob was greatly distressed to find her so sad. So he went and sat in the windowless council-chamber with the other elders and said, 'He's better than he was. Very likely, some day, we shall find him as sane as ourselves'.

Then afterwards one of the elders, who thought deeply, had an idea. He was the great doctor among these people, and the idea of curing Nunez of his peculiarities appealed to him. One day when Yacob was present he returned to the topic of Nunez.

'I have examined him,' he said, 'and the case is clearer to me. I think very probably he might be cured.'

'That is what I have always hoped,' said old Yacob.

'His brain is affected,' said the blind doctor. 'Those queer things that are called the eyes are diseased, in such a way as to affect his brain. Because of them, his brain is in a state of constant irritation and is slowly being destroyed.'

'Yes?' said old Yacob. 'Yes?'

'And I think I may say that, in order to cure him completely, all that we need do is a simple and easy surgical operation—namely, to remove his eyes.'

'And then he will be sane?'

'Then he will be perfectly sane, and a quite admirable citizen.'

'Thank heaven for science!' said old Yacob, and went at once to tell Nunez of his happy hopes.

But Nunez's manner of receiving the good news struck him as being cold and disappointing.

'One might think,' he said, 'from your manner, that you did not care for my daughter.'

It was Medina who persuaded Nunez to face the blind surgeons.

'You do not want me,' he said, 'to lose my gift of sight?'

She shook her head.

'My world is sight. There are the beautiful things, the beautiful little things—the flowers among the rocks, the far sky with its drifting clouds, the sunsets and the stars. And there is you. For you alone it is goodto have sight, to see your sweet face, your dear, beautiful hands folded together...'

'I wish,' she said, 'sometimes—' She paused.

'Yes?' said he, a little fearfully,

'I wish sometimes—you would not talk like that.'

'Like what?'

'I know it's pretty—it's your imagination. I love it, but—' He felt cold. 'But?' he said faintly.

She sat quite still.

'You mean—you think—I should be better, better perhaps—'

He was realizing things very swiftly.

'If I were to consent to this?' he said at last, in a voice that was very gentle.

She flung her arms round him, weeping wildly, 'Oh, if you would,' she sobbed, 'if only you would!'

V

For a week before the operation that was to raise him from his inferiority to the level of a blind citizen, Nunez was unable to sleep. He sat sadly while others slept, or wandered aimlessly. He had given his answer, he had given his consent, and still he was not sure.

On the last morning he had meant to go to a lonely place where the meadows were beautiful with flowers and there remain until the hour should come. But as he went he lifted up his eyes and went on, and passed through the boundary wall and out upon the rocks, and his eyes were always watching the sunlit ice and snow.

He saw their great beauty, and he thought of the free world he was parted from, the world that was his own. He thought how after a day or so one might come down through the mountains, drawing nearer and nearer to its busy streets and ways.

For example, if one went on, up that slope and to that chimney-way, then one might come out high among those pine trees that ran round on a sort of shelf. And then? Perhaps a climb might be found to take him up to the precipice that came below the snow. And then? Then one would be out upon the sun-lit snow there, and half-way up to the crest of those beautiful heights.

He glanced back at the village. He thought of Medina, and she had become small and remote.

He turned again towards the mountain wall.

Then, very slowly, he began to climb.

THE COUNTRY OF THE BLIND

About the Author

H.G. Wells, born in 1866, was first a draper's assistant and then a pupil of Huxley, the biologist. He began his literary career by writing stories with a semi-scientific flavour, based on imaginative development of some fact of science; such were **The Time Machine** (1895), **The Island of Dr. Moreau** (1896), **The Invisible man** (1897) **The war of the Worlds** (1898), and **The Food of the Gods** (1904). Here he uses the special kind of marvel which can be suggested by modern science. These ingenious tales, told in simple, vigorous language, thrill and disturb the reader with their deliberate harshness and cruelty; of all his books they have had the widest circulation at home and abroad. With the new century he began a series of novels on social themes, of which the best known are **Love and Mr. Lewisham, Kipps, The New Machiavelli and Marriage**.

Born in the lower middle rank of society and uninfluenced by the classical type of education, Wells resembles Dickens in origin, but unlike Dickens he is not content merely to make the social system more tolerable; he is ready and anxious to reconstruct the world. He sifts all conventional values and reconstructs a new world. The present piece is one such attempt.

This work is about a new world of his imagination. The Island is inhabited by blind persons. It is imaginative in appeal. He creates an imaginative world and tries to build up a contrast between the conventional world of normal people and the world of such people who are blind. In fact, he tries to go deep into the problem of existence of evil in the world. The root of evil, according to him, lies in the confusion produced by the universal rule-of thumb methods of living. What is needed is a reformation.

References

Sightless youngsters — blind children.

Outer world — some other place.

Sunlit ice — ice shining with light.

❑

THE MONKEY'S PAW

W. W. JACOB

Without, the night was cold and wet, but in the small parlour of Laburnam Villa the blinds were drawn and the fire burned brightly. Father and son were at chess, the former, who possessed ideas about the game involving radical changes, putting his king into such sharp and unnecessary perils that it even provoked comment from the white-haired old lady knitting placidly by the fire.

'Hark at the wind,' said Mr White, who, having seen a fatal mistake after it was too late, was amiably desirous of preventing his son from seeing it.

'I'm listening,' said the latter, grimly surveying the board as he stretched out his hand. 'Check.'

'I should hardly think that he'd come tonight,' said his father, with his hand poised over the board.

'Mate,' replied the son.

'That's the worst of living so far out,' bawled Mr White, with sudden and unlooked-for violence; 'of all the beastly, slushy, out-of-the-way places to live in, this is the worst. Pathway's a bog, and the road's a torrent. I don't know what people are thinking about. I suppose because only two houses in the road are let, they think it doesn't matter.'

'Never mind, dear,' said his wife, soothingly; 'perhaps you'll win the next one.'

Mr. White looked up sharply, just in time to intercept a knowing glance between mother and son. The words died away on his lips, and he hid a guilty grin in his thin grey beard.

'There he is,' said Herbert White, as the gate banged to loudly and heavy footsteps came toward the door.

The old man rose with hospitable haste, and opening the door, was heard condoling with the new arrival. The new arrival also condoled with himself, so that Mrs. White said, 'Tut, tut!' and coughed gently as her husband entered the room, followed by a tall, burly man, beady of eye and rubicund of visage.

'Sergeant-Major Morris,' he said, introducing him.

The sergeant-major shook hands, and taking the profered seat by the fire, watched contentedly while his host got out whisky and tumblers and stood a small copper kettle on the fire.

At the third glass his eyes got brighter, and he began to talk, the little family circle regarding with eager interest this visitor from distant parts, as he squared his shoulders in the chair and spoke of wild scenes and doughty deeds; of wars and plagues and strange peoples.

'Twenty-one years of it,' said Mr. White, nodding at his wife and son. 'When he went away he was a slip of a youth in the warehouse. Now look at him.'

'He don't look to have taken much harm,' said Mrs. White, politely.

'I'd like to go to India myself,' said the old man, 'just to look round a bit, you know.'

'Better where you are,' said the sergeant-major, shaking his head. He put down the empty glass, and sighing softly, shook it again.

'I should like to see those old temples and fakirs and jugglers,' said the old man. 'What was that you started telling me the other day about a monkey's paw or something, Morris?'

'Nothing,' said the soldier, hastily. 'Leastways nothing worth hearing.'

'Monkey's paw?' said Mrs White, curiously.

'Well, it's just a bit of what you might call magic, perhaps,' said the sergeant-major, off handedly.

His three listeners leaned forward eagerly. The visitor absent-mindedly put his empty glass to his lips and then set it down again. His host filled it for him.

'To look at,' said the sergeant-major, fumbling in his pocket, 'it's just an ordinary little paw, dried to a mummy.'

He took something out of his pocket and proffered it. Mrs. White drew back with a grimace, but her son, taking it, examined it curiously.

'And what is there special about it?' inquired Mr. White as he took it from his son, and having examined it, placed it upon the table.

'It had a spell put on it by an old fakir,' said the sergeant-major, 'a very holy man. He wanted to show that fate ruled people's lives, and that those who interfered with it did so to their sorrow. He put a spell on it so that three separate men could each have three wishes from it.'

His manner was so impressive that his hearers were conscious that their light laughter jarred somewhat.

'Well, why don't you have three, sir?' said Herbert White, cleverly.

The soldier regarded him in the way that middle age is wont to regard presumptuous youth. 'I have,' he said, quietly, and his blotchy face whitened.

'And did you really have the three wishes granted?' asked Mrs. White.

'I did,' said the sergeant-major, and his glass tapped against his strong teeth.

'And has anybody else wished?' persisted the old lady.

'The first man had his three wishes. Yes,' was the reply; 'I don't know what the first two were, but the third was for death. That's how I got the paw.'

His tones were so grave that a hush fell upon the group.

'If you've had your three wishes, it's no good to you now, then, Morris,' said the old man at last. 'What do you keep it for?'

The soldier shook his head. 'Fancy, I suppose,' he said, slowly. 'I did have some idea of selling it, but I don't think I will. It has caused enough mischief already. Besides, people won't buy. They think it's a fairy tale; some of them, and those who do think anything of it want to try it first and pay me afterward.'

'If you could have another three wishes,' said the old man, eyeing him keenly, 'would you have them?'

'I don't know,' said the other. 'I don't know.'

He took the paw, and dangling it between his forefinger and thumb, suddenly threw it upon the fire. White, with a slight cry, stooped down and snatched it off.

'Better let it burn,' said the soldier, solemnly.

'If you don't want it, Morris,' said the other, 'give it to me.'

'I won't,' said his friend, doggedly. 'I threw it on the fire. If you keep it, don't blame me for what happens. Pitch it on the fire again like a sensible man.'

The other shook his head and examined his new possession closely. 'How do you do it?' he inquired.

'Hold it up in your right hand and wish aloud,' said the sergeant-major, 'but I warn you of the consequences.'

'Sounds like the *Arabian Nights*,' said Mrs White, as she rose and began to set the supper. 'Don't you think you might wish for four pairs of hands for me?'

Her husband drew the talisman from pocket, and then all three burst into laughter as the sergeant-major, with a look of alarm on his face, caught him by the arm.

'If you must wish,' he said gruffly, 'wish for something sensible.'

Mr. White dropped it back in his pocket, and placing chairs, motioned his friend of supper the talisman was partly forgotten, and afterward the three sat listening in an enthralled fashion to a second instalment of the soldier's adventures in India.

'If the tale about the monkey's paw is not more truthful than those he has been telling us,' said Herbert, as the door closed behind their guest, just in time for him to catch the last train, 'we sha'nt make much out of it.'

'Did you give him anything for it, father?' inquired Mrs White, regarding her husband closely.

'A trifle,' said he, colouring slightly. 'He didn't want it, but I made him take it. And he pressed me again to throw it away.'

'Likely,' said Herbert, with pretended horror. 'Why, we're going to be rich, and famous and happy. Wish to be an emperor, father, to begin with; then you can't be henpecked.'

He darted round the table. pursued by the maligned Mrs. White armed with an antimacassar.

Mr. White took the paw from his pocket and eyed it dubiously. 'I don't know what to wish for, and that' a fact,' he said, slowly. 'It seems to me I've got all I want.'

'If you only cleared the house, you'd be quite happy, wouldn't you?' said Herbert, with his hand on his shoulder. 'Well, wish for two hundred pounds, then; that'll just do it.'

His father, smiling shamefacedly at his own credulity, held up the talisman, as his son, with a solemn face, some-what married by a wink at his mother, sat down at the piano and struck a few impressive chords.

'I wish for two hundred pounds,' said the old man distinctly.

A fine crash from the piano greeted the words, interrupted by a shuddering cry from the old man. His wife and son ran toward him.

'It moved,' he cried, with a glance of disgust at the object as it lay on the floor. 'As I wished, it twisted in my hand like a snake.'

'Well, I don't see the money,' said his son as he picked it up and placed it on the table, 'and I bet I never shall.'

'It must have been your fancy, father,' said his wife, regarding him anxiously.

He shook his head. 'Never mind, though; there's no harm done, but it gave me a shock all the same.'

They sat down by the fire again while the two men finished their pipes. Outside, the wind was higher than ever, and the old man started nervously at the sound of a door banging upstairs. A silence unusual and depressing settled upon all three, which lasted unti the old couple rose to retire for the night.

'I expect you'll find the cash tied up in a big bag in the middle of your bed,' said Herbert, as he bade them good night, 'and something horrible squatting up on top of the wardrobe watching you as you pocket your ill-gotten gains.'

He sat alone in the darkness, gazing at the dying fire, and seeing faces in it. The last face was so horrible and so simian that he gazed at it in amazement. It got so vivid that, with a little uneasy laugh, he felt on the table for a glass containing a little water to throw over it. His hand grasped the monkey's paw, and with a little shiver he wiped his hand on his coat and went up to bed.

II

In the brightness of the wintry sun next morning as it streamed over the breakfast table he laughed at his fears. There was an air of prosaic wholesomeness about the room which it had lacked on the previous night, and the dirty, shrivelled little paw was pitched on the sideboard with a carelessness which betokened no great belief in its virtues.

'I suppose all old soldiers are the same,' said Mrs White. 'The idea of our listening to such nonsense! How could wishes be granted in these days? And if they could how could two hundred pounds hurt you, father?'

'Might drop on his head from the sky,' said the frivolous Herbert.

'Morris said the things happened so naturally,' said his father, 'that you might if you so wished attribute it to coincidence.'

'Well, don't break into the money before I come back,' said Herbert as he rose from the table. 'I'm afraid it'll turn you into a mean, avaricious man, and we shall have to disown you.'

His mother laughed, and following him to the door, watched him down the road; and returning to the breakfat table, was very happy at the expense of her husband's credulity. All of which did not prevent her from scurrying to the door at the postman's knock, nor prevent her from referring somewhat shortly to retired sergeant-majors of bibulous habits when she found that the post brought a tailor's bill.

'Herbert will have some more of his funny remarks, I expect, when he comes home,' she said, as they sat at dinner.

'I dare say,' said Mr. White, pouring himself out some beer; 'but for all that, the thing moved in my hand; that I'll swear to.'

'You thought it did,' said the old lady soothingly.

'I say it did,' replied the other. 'There was no thought about it; I had just–What's the matter?'

His wife made no reply. She was watching the mysterious movements of a man outside, who, peering in an undecided fashion at the house, appeared to be trying to make up his mind to enter. In mental connexion with the two hundred pounds, she noticed that the stranger was well dressed, and wore a silk hat of glossy newness. Three times he paused at the gate, and then walked on again. The fourth time he stood with his hand upon it, and then with sudden resolution flung it open and walked up the path. Mrs. White at the same moment placed her hands behind her, and hurriedly unfastening the strings of her apron, put that useful article of apparel beneath the cushion of her chair.

She brought the stranger, who seemed ill at ease, into the room. He gazed at her furtively, and listened in a preoccupied fashion as the old lady apologized for the appearance of the room, and her husband's coat, a garment which he usually reserved for the garden.' She then waited as patiently as her sex would permit, for him to broach his business, but he was at first strangely silent.

'I—was asked to call,' he said at last, and stooped and picked a piece of cotton from his trousers. 'I come from Maw and Meggins.'

The old lady started. 'Is anything the matter?' she asked, breathlessly. 'Has anything happened to Herbert? What is it? What is it?'

Her husband interposed. 'There, there, mother,' he said, hastily. 'Sit down, and don't jump to conclusions. You've not brought bad news, I'm sure, sir'; and he eyed the other wistfully.

'I'm sorry—' began the visitor.

'Is he hurt?' demanded the mother, wildly.

The visitor bowed in assent. 'Badly hurt,' he said, quietly, 'but he is not in any pain.'

'Oh, thank God!' said the old woman, clasping her hands. 'Thank God for that! Thank—'

She broke off suddenly as the sinister meaning of the assurance dawned upon her and she saw the awful confirmation of her fears in the other's averted face. She caught her breath, and turning to her slower-witted husband, laid her trembling old hand upon his. There was a long silence.

'He was caught in the machinery,' said the visitor at length in a low voice.

'Caught in the machinery,' repeated Mr. White, in a dazed fashion, 'yes.'

He sat staring blankly out at the window, and taking his wife's hand between his own, pressed it as he had been wont to do in their old courting-days nearly forty years before.

'He was the only one left to us,' he said, turning gently to the visitor. 'It is hard.'

The other coughed, and rising, walked slowly to the window. 'The firm wished me to convey their sincere sympathy with you in your great loss,' he said, without looking round. 'I beg that you will understand I am only their servant and merely obeying orders.'

There was no reply; the old woman's face was white, her eyes staring, and her breath inaudible; on the husband's face was a look such as his friend the sergeant might have carried into his first action.

'I was to say that Maw and Meggins disclaim all responsibility,' continued the other. 'They admit no liability at all, but in consideration of your son's services, they wish to present you with a certain sum as compensation.'

Mr. White dropped his wife's hand, and rising to his feet, gazed with a look of horror at his visitor. His dry lips shaped the words, 'How much?'

'Two hundred pounds,' was the answer.

Unconscious of his wife's shriek, the old man smiled faintly, put out his hands like a sightless man, and dropped, a senseless heap, to the floor.

III

In the huge new cemetery, some two miles distant, the old people buried their dead, and came back to a house steeped in shadow and silence. It was all over so quickly that at first they could hardly realize it, and remained in a state of expectation as though of something else to happen-something else which was to lighten this load, too heavy for old hearts to bear.

But the days passed, and expectation gave place to resignation – the hopeless resignation of the old, sometimes miscalled apathy. Sometimes they hardly exchanged a word, for now they had nothing to talk about, and their days were long to weariness.

It was about a week after that the old man, waking suddenly in the night, stretched out his hand and found himself alone. The room was in darkness, and the sound of subdued weeping came from the window. He raised himself in bed and listened.

'Come back,' he said, tenderly. 'You will be cold.'

'It is colder for my son,' said the old woman, and wept afresh.

The sound of her sobs died away on his ears. The bed was warm, and his eyes heavy with sleep. He dozed fitfully, and then slept until a sudden wild cry from his wife awoke him with a start.

'*The paw* !' she cried wildly. 'The monkey's paw!'

He started up in alarm. 'Where? Where is it? What's the matter?'

She came stumbling across the room toward him. 'I want it,' she said, quietly. 'You've not destroyed it?'

'It's in the parlour, on the bracket,' he replied, marveling. 'Why?'

She cried and laughed together, and bending over, kissed his cheek.

'I only just thought of it,' she said, hysterically. 'Why didn't I think of it before? Why didn't you think of it?'

'Think of what?' he questioned.

'The other two wishes,' she replied, rapidly. 'We've only had one.'

'Was not that enough?' he demanded, fiercely.

'No,' she cried triumphantly; 'we'll have one more. Go down and get it quickly, and wish our boy alive again.'

The man sat up in bed and flung the bedclothes from his quaking limbs. 'Good Good, you are mad!' he cried, aghast.

'Get it,' she panted; 'get it quickly, and wish–Oh, my boy, my boy!'

Her husband struck a match and lit the candle. 'Get back to bed,' he said, unsteadily. 'You don't know what you are saying.'

'We had the first wish granted,' said the old woman, feverishly; 'why not the second?'

'A coincidence,' stammered the old man.

'Go and get it and wish,' cried his wife, quivering with excitement.

The old man turned and regarded her, and his voice shook. 'He has been dead ten days, and besides he—I would not tell you else, but—I could only recognize him by his clothing. If he was too terrible for you to see then, how now?'

'Bring him back?' cried the old woman, and dragged him toward the door. 'Do you think I fear the child I have nursed?'

He went down in the darkness, and felt his way to the parlour, and then to the mantelpiece. The talisman was in its place, and a horrible fear that the unspoken wish might bring his mutilated son before him ere he could escape from the room seized upon him, and he caught his breath as he found that he had lost the direction of the door. His brow cold with sweat, he felt his way round the table, and groped along the wall until he found himself in the small passage with the unwholesome thing in his hand.

Even his wife's face seemed changed as he entered the room. It was white and expectant, and to his fears seemed to have an unnatural look upon it. He was afraid of her.

'*Wish* !' she cried, in a strong voice.

'It is foolish and wicked,' he faltered.

'*Wish* !' repeated his wife.

He raised his hand. 'I wish my son alive again.'

The talisman fell to the floor, and he regarded it fearfully. Then he sank trembling into a chair as the old woman, with burning eyes, walked to the window and raised the blind.

He sat until he was chilled with the cold, glancing occasionally at the figure of the old woman peering through the window. The candle-end, which had burned below the rim of the china candlestick, was throwing pulsating shadows on the ceiling and walls, until, with a flicker larger than the rest, it expired. The old man, with an unspeakable sense of relief at the failure of the talisman, crept back to his bed, and in a minute or two afterward the old woman came silently and apathetically beside him.

Neither spoke, but lay silently listening to the ticking of the clock. A stair creaked, and a squeaky mouse scuried noisily through the wall. The darkness was oppressive, and after lying for sometime screwing up his courage, he took the box of matches, and striking one, went downstairs for a candle.

At the foot of the stairs the match went out, and he paused to strike another; and at the same moment a knock, so quiet and stealthy as to be scarcely audible, sounded on the front door.

The matches fell from his hand and spilled in the passage. He stood motionless, his breath suspended until the knock was repeated. Then he turned and fled swiftly back to his room, and closed the door behind him. A third knock sounded through the house.

'*What's that?*' cried the old woman, starting up.

'A rat,' said the old man in shaking tones — 'a rat. It passed me on the stairs.'

His wife sat up in bed listening. A loud knock resounded through the house.

It's Herbert!' she screamed. 'It's Herbert!'

She ran to the door, but her husband was before her, and catching her by the arm, held her tightly.

'What are you going to do?' he whispered hoarsely.

'It's my boy; it's Herbert!' she cried, struggling mechanically. 'I forgot it was two miles away. What are you holding me for? Let go. I must open the door.

'For God's sake don't let it in,' cried the old man, trembling.

'You're afraid of your own son,' she cried, struggling. 'Let me go. I'm coming, Herbert; I'm coming.'

There was another knock, and another. The old woman with a sudden wrench broke free and ran from the room. Her husband followed to the landing, and called after her appealingly as she hurried downstairs. He heard the chain rattle back and the bottom bolt drawn slowly and stiffly from the socket. Then the old woman's voice, strained and painting.

'The bolt,' she cried, loudly. 'Come down. I can't reach it.'

But her husband was on his knees groping wildly on the floor in search of the paw. If he could only find it before the thing outside got in. A perfect fusillade of knocks reverberated through the house, and he heard the scraping of a chair as his wife put it down in the passage against the door. He heard the creaking of the bolt as it came slowly back, and at the same moment he found the monkey's paw, and frantically breathed his third and last wish.

The knocking ceased suddenly, although the echoes of it were still in the house. He heard the chair drawn back, and the door opened A cold wind rushed up the staircase, and a long loud wail of disappointment and misery from his wife gave him courage to run down to her side, and then to the gate beyond. The street lamp flickering opposite shone on a quiet and deserted road.

THE MONEKY'S PAW

About the Author

William Waymark Jacob was born in Wapping, East London, in 1863. His father was a warf manager and the boy grew up among the Longshoremen and other dockland characters who were to figure so prominently in his short stories.

In 1883 he entered the Savings Bank Department of the Civil Service, where he remained as a clerk until 1899. Long before then he had begun to make his mark as a humorous writer under the wing of Jerome K. Jerome in the Pages of **The Idler** and **Today** and **Later** in the **Strand Magazine**. **Many Cargoes,** his first volume of short stories, was published in 1896; but it was not until the publication of his third book, three years later, that Jacob decided to adopt writing as a profession and success followed successes as he published, more than twenty volumes; most of them collection of short stories, until his death in 1943.

The humour of W. W. Jacob is in the masculine English tradition which immortalizes the comic characters of Shakespeare, Dickens and the Grossmiths. Almost all his short stories are concerned with the warf life he knew so well in the London of four-wheelers, music halls, magic lantern shows and Threepeny beer in the Mile End Road, night watchman had a fund of tales about the advanture of Sam small, Ginger Dick, and Peter Russet, who generally share a room in a seamen's Lodging house when they come ashore with pockets full of money.

In the famous and compelling story the 'Monkey's Paw' and also in 'The Well' Jacob shows his craftmanship in evoking the uncanny.

The rich characterization, largely revealed through dialogue, indicates a shrewd understanding of human motives; and the narrative power is masterly. This piece the 'Monkey's Paw' has a double appeal; as a period piece, and as perenial comedy. His stories have been immensely popular. His tales are masterpieces of taut, uncanny narrative, and the evidence of their credibility which the author provides is disconcertingly pursuasive.

There is a scholarly precision in the style, an academic reticence, which gives the various revelations a small whispering horror unequalled else where.

❑

THE DOLL'S HOUSE

KATHERINE MANSFIELD

When dear old Mrs. Hay went back to town after staying with the Burnells she sent the children a doll's house. It was so big that the carter and Pat carried it into the courtyard, and there it stayed, propped up on two wooden boxes beside the feed-room door. No harm could come to it; it was summer. And perhaps the smell of paint would have gone off by the time it had to be taken in. For, really, the smell of paint coming from that doll's house ('Sweet of old Mrs. Hay, of course; most sweet and generous!')—but the smell of paint was quite enough to make anyone seriously ill, in Aunt Beryl's opion. Even before the sacking was taken off. And when it was . . .

There stood the doll's house, a dark, oily, spinach green, picked out with bright yellow. Its two solid little chimneys, glued on to the roof, were painted red and white, and the door, gleaming with yellow varnish, was like a little slab of toffee. Four windows, real windows, were divided into pones by a broad streak of green. There was actually a tiny porch, too, painted yellow, with big lumps of congealed paint hanging along the edge.

But perfect, perfect little house! Who could possibly mind the smell. It was part of the joy, part of the newness.

'Open it quickly, someone!'

The hook at the side was stuck fast. Pat prised it open with his penknife, and the whole house fron swung back, and—there you were, gazing at one and the same moment into the drawing-room and dining-room, the kitchen and two bedrooms. That is the house for a way to open! Why don't all houses open like that? How much more exciting than peering through the slit of a door into a mean little hall with a hat-stand and two umbrellas! That is—isn't it?—what you long to know about a house when you put your hand on the knocker. Perhaps it is the way God opens houses at the dead of night when He is taking a quiet turn with an angle . . .

'Oh-oh!' The Burnell children sounded as though they were in despair.

It was too marvellous; it was too much for them. They had never seen anything like it in their lives. All the rooms were papered. There were pictures on the walls, painted on the paper, with gold frames complete. Red carpet covered all the floors except the kitchen; red plush chairs in the drawing-room, green in the dining-room; tables, beds with real bed-clothes, a cradle, a stove, a dresser with tiny plates and one big jug. But what Kezia liked more than anything, what she liked frightfully, was the lamp. It stood in the middle, of the dining-room table, an exquisite little amber lamp with a white globe. It was even filled all ready for lighting, though, of course, you couldn't light it. But there was something inside that looked like oil and moved when you shook it.

The father and mother dolls, who sprawled very stiff as though they had fainted in the drawing-room, and their two little children asleep upstairs, were really too big for the doll's house. They didn't look as though they belonged to it. But the lamp was perfect. It seemed to smile at Kezia, to say, 'I live here.' The lamp was real.

The Burnell children could hardly walk to school fast enough the next morning. They burned to tell everybody to describe, to—well—to boast about their doll's house before the schoolbell rang.

'I'm to tell,' said Isabel, 'because I'm the eldest. And you two can join in after. But I'm to tell first.'

There was nothing to answer. Isabel was bossy, but she was always right, and Lottie and Kezia knew too well the powers that went with being eldest. They brushed through the thick buttercups at the road edge and said nothing.

'And I'm to choose who's to come and see it first. Mother said I might.'

For it had been arranged that while the doll's house stood in the courtyard they might ask the girls at school, two at a time, to come and look. Not to stay to tea, of course, or to come traipsing through the house. But just to stand quietly in the courtyard while Isabel pointed out the beauties, and Lottie and Kezia looked pleased . . .

But hurry as they might, by the time they reached the tarred palings of the boys' playground the bell had begun to jangle. They only just had time to whip off then hats and fall into line before the roll was called. Never mind. Isabel tried to make up forit by looking very important and mysterious and by whispering behind her hand to the girls near her, 'Got something to tell you at playtime.'

Playtime came and Isabel was surrounded. The girls of her class nearly fought to put their arms round her to walk away with her, to beam flatteringly, to be her special friend. She held quite a court under the huge pine trees at the side of the playground. Nudging, giggling together, the little girls pressed up close. And the only two who stayed outside the ring were the two who were always outside, the little Kelveys. They knew better than to come anywhere near the Burnells.

For the fact was, the school the Burnell children went to was not at all the kind of place their parents would have chosen if there had been any choice. But there was none. It was the only school for miles. And the consequence was all the children of the neighbourhood, the Judge's little girls, the doctor's daughters, the storekeeper's children, the milkman's, were forced to mix together. Not to speak of there being an equal number of rude, rough little boys as well. But the line had to be drawn somewhere. It was drawn at the Kelveys. Many of the children, including the Burnells, were not allowed even to speak to them. They walked past the Kelveys with their heads in the air, and as they set the fashion in all matters of behaviour, the Kelveys were shunned by everybody. Even the teacher had a special voice for them, and a special smile for the other children when Lil Kelvey came up to her desk with a bunch of dreadfully common-looking flowers.

They were the daughters of a spry, hard-working little washerwoman, who went about from house to house by the day. This was awful enough. But where was Mr. Kelvey? Nobody knew for certain. But everybody said he was in prison. So they were the daughters of a washerwoman and a gaolbird. Very nice company for other people's children! And they looked it. Why Mrs. Kelvey made them so conspicuous was hard to understand. The truth was they were dressed in 'bits' given to her by the people for whom she worked. Lil, for instance, who was a stout, plain child, with big freckles, came to school in a dress made from a green art-serge tablecloth of the Burnells, with red plush sleeves from the Logan's curtains. Her hat, perched on top of her high forehead, was a grown-up woman's hat, once the property of Miss Lecky, the postmistress. It was turned up at the back and trimmed with a large scarlet quill. What a little guy she looked! It was impossible not to laugh, And her little sister, our Else, wore a long white dress, rather like a nightgown, and a pair of little boy's boots.

But whatever our Else wore she would have looked stange. She was a tiny wishbone of a child, with cropped hair and enormous solemn eyes—a little white owl. Nobody had ever seen her smile; she scarcely ever spoke. She went through life holding on to Lil, with a piece of Lil's skirt screwed up in her hand. Where Lil went, our Else followed. In the playground, on the road going to and from school, there was Lil marching in front and our Else holding on behind. Only when she wanted anything. or when she was out of breath, our Else gave Lil a tug, a twitch, and Lil stopped and turned round. The Kelveys never failed to understand each other.

Now they hovered at the edge; you couldn't stop them listening. When the little girls turned round and sneered, Lil, as usual, gave her silly, shamefaced smile, but our Else only looked.

And Isabel's voice, so very proud, went on telling.

The carpet made a great sensation, but so did the beds with real bedclothes, and the stove with an oven door.

When she finished Kezia broke in. You've forgotten the lamp, Isabel.'

'Oh yes,' said Isabel, 'and there's a teeny little lamp, all made of yellow glass, with a white globe that stands on the dining-room table. You couldn't tell it from a real one.'

'The lamp's best of all,' cried Kezia. She thought Isabel wasn't making half enough of the little lamp. But nobody paid any attention. Isable was choosing the two who were to come back with them that afternoon and see it. She chose Emmie Cole and Lena Logan. But when the others knew they were all to have a chance, they couldn't be nice enough to Isabel. One by one they put their arms round Isabel's waist and walked her off. They had something to whisper to her, a secret. 'Isabel's my friend.'

Only the little Kelveys moved away forgotten; there was nothing more for them to hear.

Days passed, and as more children saw the doll's house, the fame of it spread. It became the one subject, the rage. The one question was, 'Have you seen Burnells' doll's house? Oh, ain't it lovely!' 'Haven't you seen it? Oh, I say!'

Even the dinner hour was given up to talking about it. The little girls sat under the pines eatng their thick mutton sandwiches and big slabs of johnny cake spread with butter. While always, as near as they could get, sat the Kelveys, our Else holding on to Lil, litening too, while they chewed their jam sandwiches out of a newspaper soaked with large red blobs.

'Mother,' said Kezia, 'can't I ask the Kelveys just once?'

'Certainly not, Kezia.'

'But why not ?'

'Run away, Kezia; you know quite well why not.'

At last everybody had seen it except them. On that day the subject rather flagged. It was the dinner hour. The children stood together under the pine trees, and suddenly, as they looked at the Kelveys, eating out of their paper, always by themselves, always listening, they wanted to be horried to them. Emmie Cole started the whisper.

'Lil Kelvey's going to be a servant when she grows up.'

'O-oh, how awful!' said Isabel Burnell, and she made eyes at Emmie.

Emmie swallowed in a very meaning way and nodded to Isabel as she'd seen her mother do on those occasions.

'It's true—it's true—it's true,' she said.

Then Lena Logan's little eyes snapped. 'Shall I ask her?' she whispered.

'Bet you don't,' said Jessie May.

'Pooh, I'm not frightened,' said Lena. Suddenly she gave a little squeal and danced in front of the other girls. 'Watch! Watch me! Watch me now!' said Lena And sliding, gliding, dragging one foot, giggling behind her hand, Lena went over to the Kelveys.

Lil looked up from her dinner. She wrapped the rest quickly away. Our Else stopped chewing. What was coming now?

'Is it true you're going to be a servant when you grow up, Lil Kelvey?' shrilled Lena.

Dead silence. But instead of answering, Lil only gave her silly, shamefaced smile. She didn't seem to mind the question at all. What a sell for Lena! The girls began to titter.

Lena couldn't stand that. She put her hands on her hips; she shot forward. 'Yah, yer father's in prison!' she hissed spitefully.

This was such a marvellous thing to have said that the little girls rushed away in a body, deeply, deeply excited, wild with joy. Someone found a long rope, and they began skipping. And never did they skip so high, run in and out so fast, or do such daring things as on that morning.

In the afternoon Pat called for the Burnell children with the buggy and they drove home. There were visitors. Isabel and Lottie, who liked visitors, went upstairs to change their pinafores. But Kezia thieved out at the back.

Nobody was about; she began to swing on the big white gates of the courtyard. Presently, looking along the road, she saw two little dots. They grew bigger, they were coming towards her. Now she could see that they were the Kelveys. Kezia stopped swinging. She slipped off the gate as if she was going to run away. Then she hesitated. The Kelveys came nearer and beside them walked their shadows, very long, stretching right across the road with their heads in the buttercups. Kezia clambered back on the gate; she had made up her mind; she swung out.

'Hullo,' she said to the passing Kelveys.

They were so astounded that they stopped. Lil gave her silly smile. Our Else stared.

'You can come and see our doll's house if you want to,' said Kezia, and she dragged one toe on the ground. But at that Lil turned red and shook her head quickly.

'Why not?' asked Kezia.

Lil gasped, then she said, 'Your ma told our ma you wasn't to speak to us.'

'Oh, well,' said Kezia. She didn't know what to reply. 'It doesn't matter. You can come and see our doll's house all the same. Come on, Nobody's looking.'

But Lil shook her head still harder.

'Don't you want to?' asked Kezia.

Suddenly there was a twitch, a tug at Lil's skirt. She turned round. Our Else was looking at her with big, imploring eyes; she was frowning; she wanted to go. For a moment Lil looked at our Else very doubtfully. But then our Else twitched her skirt again. She started forward. Kezia led the way. Like two little stray cats they followed across the courtyard to where the doll's house stood.

'There it is,' said Kezia.

There was a pause. Lil breathed loudly, almost snorted; our Else was still as stone.

'I'll open it for you,' said Kezia kindly. She undid the hook and they looked inside.

'There's the drawing-room and the dining-room, and that's the ...'

'Kezia!'

Oh, what a start they gave !

'Kezia!'

It was Aunt Beryl's voice. They turned round. At the back door stood Aunt Beryl, staring as if she couldn't believe what she saw.

'How dare you ask the little Kelveys into the courtyard!' said her cold, furious voice. 'You know as well as I do, you're not allowed to talk to them. Run away, children, run away at once. And don't come back again,' said Aunt Beryl. And she stepped into the yard and shooed them out as if they were chickens.

'Off you go immediately!' she called, cold and proud.

They did not need telling twice. Burning with shame, shrinking together, Lil huddling along like her mother, our Else dazed, somehow they crossed the big courtyard and squeezed through the white gate.

'Wicked, disobedient little girl!' said Aunt Beryl bitterly to Kezia, and she slammed the doll's house too.

The afternoon had been awful. A letter had come from Willie Brent, a terrifying, threatening letter, saying if she did not meet him that evening in Pulman's Bush, he'd come to the front door and ask the reason why! But now that she had frightened those little rats of Kelveys and given Kezia a good scolding, her heart felt lighter. That ghastly pressure was gone. She went back to the house humming.

When the Kelveys were well out of sight of Burnells' they sat down to rest on a big red drainpipe by the side of the road. Lil's cheeks were still burning: she took off the hat with the quill and held it on her knee. Dreamily they looked over the hay paddocks, past the creek, to the group of wattles where Logan's cows stood waiting to be milked. What were their thoughts?

Presently our Else nudged up close to her sister. But now she had forgotten the cross lady. She put out a finger and stroked her sister's quill; she smiled her rare smile.

'I seen the little lamp,' she said softly,

Then both were silent once more.

THE DOLL'S HOUSE

About the Author

Kathrine Mansfield (Beauchamp) 1889–1923) born in Newzealand, married to the famous critic John Middletin Murry, is an accomplished short stroy writer. This most delicate Newzealand leterary talent matured and wrote with a European stance. Her stories are in the classical tradition. They reflect emotions and the unrest of the period. Writing under the influence of Colete, Proust and Chekhov her unerring intuition in human nature, specially of children set her apart. Her language shares her commitment to perfection. There is a pronounced wittiness, tenderness and humour in her delineation of children and animal world. The greatest achievement of short stories are—truth, a sense of wonder, unexpected freshness and poignancy.

"The Doll's House" is a famous short story written by Katharine Mansfield in which the psyche of the little children Kezia Burnell and the Kelvys have been delicately handled. Kelvys are shunned because they are the washerwoman's children. Lill kelvy when she grew up will be a servant like her mother. Though Burnells have to attend the same school, they must keep a distance. But this relationship is disturbed when the Burnell Children have been presented a beautiful doll's house. It is life like and soon becomes the centre of attraction of the children of this quiet country. All children come and peep into the house and even touch it except the poor Kelvys. Kezia wanted to invite them but is fobidden. Yet Kezia on a quiet afternoon asks Else and Lil to see her Doll's house. They come like two stray cats. While they are lost in their admiration, Mrs. Burnel's voice frightens them and they run away; Kezia has broken the understanding and is the disobedient one. Her feelings are significant part of the story. The Kelvys may be frightened out of their wit but afterall they have seen the little lamp.

❑

THE SELFISH GIANT

OSCAR WILDE

Every afternoon, as they were coming from school the children used to go and play in the Giant's garden.

It was a large, lovely garden, with soft green grass. Here and there over the grass stood beautiful flowers like stars, and there were twelve peach-trees that in the spring-time broke out into delicate blossoms of pink and pearl, and in the autumn bore rich fruit. The birds sat on the trees and sang so sweetly that the children used to stop their games in order to listen to them. "How happy we are here!" they cried to each other.

One day the Giant came back. He had been to visit his friend the Cornish ogre, and had stayed with him for seven years. After the seven years were over he had said all that he had to say, for his conversation was limited and he determined to return to his own castle. When he arrived he saw the children playing in the garden.

"What are you doing there?" he cried in a very gruff voice, and the children ran away.

"My own garden is my own garden," said the Giant; "any one can understand that, and I will allow nobody to play in it but myself." So he built a high wall all round it, and put up a notice-board—

TRESPASSERS

WILL BE

PROSECUTED

He was a very selfish Giant.

The poor children had now nowhere to play. They tried to play on the road, but the road was very dusty and full of hard stones, and they did not like it. They used to wander round the high wall when their lessons were over, and talk about the beautiful garden inside, "How happy we were there," they said to each other.

Then the Spring came and all over the country there were little blossoms and little birds. Only in the garden of the Selfish Giant it was still winter. The birds did not care to sing in it, as there were no children, and the trees forgot to blossom. Once a beautiful flower put its head out from the grass, but when it saw the notice-borad it was so sorry for the children that it slipped back into the ground again, and went off to sleep. The only people who were pleased were the Snow and the Frost. "Spring has forgotten this garden," they cried, "so we will live here all the year round." The Snow covered up the grass with her great white cloak, and the Frost painted all the trees silver. Then they invited the North Wind to stay with them, and he came. He was wrapped in furs, and he roared all day about the garden, and blew the chimney-pots down. "This is a delightful spot," he said; "we must ask the Hail on a visit." So the Hail came. Every day for three hours he rattled on the roof of the castle till he broke most of the slates, and then he ran round and round the garden as fast as he could go. He was dressed in grey, and his breath was like ice.

"I cannot understand why the Spring is so late in coming," said the Selfish Giant, as he sat at the window and looked out at his cold, white garden; "I hope there will be a change in the weather."

But the Spring never came, nor the Summer. The Autumn gave golden fruit to every garden, but to the Giant's garden she gave none. "He is too selfish," she said. So it was always Winter there, and the North Wind, and the Hail, and the Frost, and the Snow danced about through the trees.

One morning the Giant was lying awake in bed when he heard some lovely music. It sounded so sweet to his ears that he thought it must be the King's musician passing by. It was really only a little linnet singing outside his window, but it was so long since he had heard a bird sing in his garden that it seemed to him to be the most beautiful music in the world. Then the Hail stopped dancing over his head, and the North Wind ceased roaring and a delicious perfume came to him through the open casement. "I believe the Spring has come at last," said the Giant; and he jumped out of bed and looked out.

What did he see?

He saw a most wonderful sight. Through a little hole in the wall the children had crept in, and they were sitting in the branches of the trees. In every tree that he could see there was a little child. And the trees were so glad to have the children back again that they had covered themselves with blossoms, and were waving their arms gently above the children's heads. The birds were flying about and twittering with delight, and the flowers were looking up through the green grass and laughing. It was a lovely scene; only in one corner it was still winter. It was the farthest corner of the garden, and in it was standing a little boy. He was so small that he could not reach up to the branches of the tree, and he was wandering all round it, crying bitterly. The poor tree was still quite covered with frost and snow, and the North Wind was blowing and roaring above it. "Climb up, little boy," said the Tree, and it bent its branches as low as it could; but the boy was too tiny.

And the Giant's heart melted as he looked out. "How selfish I have been!" he said. "Now I know why the Spring would not come here. I will put that poor little boy on the top of the tree, and then I will knock down the wall, and my garden shall be the children's playground for ever and ever." He was really very sorry for what he had done.

So he crept downstairs and opened the front door quite softly, and went out into the garden. But when the children saw him they were so frightened that they all ran away, and the garden became winter again. Only the little boy did not run, for his eyes were so full of tears that he did not see the Giant coming. And the Giant stole up behind him and took him gently in his hand, and put him into the tree. And the tree broke at once into blossoms, and the birds came and sang on it, and the little boy stretched out his two arms and flung them round the Giant's neck and kissed him. And the other children, when they saw that the Giant was not wicked any longer, came running back, and with them came the Spring. "It is your garden now, little children," said the Giant, and he took a great axe and knocked down the wall. And when the people were going to market at twelve o'clock they found the Giant playing with the children in the most beautiful garden they had ever seen.

All day long they played, and in the evening they came to the Giant to bid him good-bye.

"But where is your little companion?" he said; "the boy I put into the tree." The Giant loved him the best because he had kissed him.

"We don't know," answered the children; "he has gone away."

"You must tell him to be sure and come here tomorrow," said the Giant. But the children said that they did not know where he lived, and had never seen him before; and the Giant felt very sad.

Every afternoon, when school was over, the children came and played with the Giant. But the little boy whom the Giant loved was never seen again. The Giant was very kind to all the children, yet he longed for his first little friend, and often spoke of him. "How I would like to see him!" he used to say.

Years went over, and the Giant grew very old and feeble. He could not play about any more, so he sat in a huge armchair and watched the children at their games, and admired his garden. "I have many beautiful flowers," he said; "but the children are the most beautiful flowers of all."

One winter morning he looked out of his window as he was dressing. He did not hate the winter now, for he knew that it was merely the Spring asleep, and that the flowers were resting.

Suddenly he rubbed his eyes in wonder, and looked and looked. It certainly was a marvellous sight. In the farthest corner of the garden was a tree quite covered with lovely white blossoms. Its branches were all golden and silver fruit hung down from them, and underneath it stood the little boy he had loved.

Downstairs ran the Giant in great joy, and out into the garden. He hastened across the grass, and came near to the child. And when he came quite close his face grew red with anger, and he said, "Who hath dared to wound thee?" For on the palms of the child's hands were the prints of two nails, and the prints of two nails were on the little feet.

"Who hath dared to wound thee?" cried the Giant; "tell me, that I may take my big sword and slay him."

"Nay!" answered the child; "but these are the wounds of Love."

"Who art thou?" said the Giant, and a strange awe fell on him, and her knelt before the little child.

And the child smiled on the Giant, and said to him, "You let me play once in your garden, to-day you shall come with me to my garden, which is Paradise."

And when the children ran in that afternoon, they found the Giant lying dead under the tree, all covered with white blossoms.

THE SELFISH GIANT

About the Author

Oscar Wilde (1854–1900) is an Irish story writer and playwright. He was born and brought up in Dublin, where he went to Trenity college,

Dublin. He moved to Oxford and began the cult of 'aestheticism' and was caricatured by "Punch" a famous magazine of the time. His literary life came abruptly to an end when was imprisoned for homosexuality, which was an activity neither understood nor tolerated at that time. He was imprisoned and died shortly.

This story is based on St. Mark 10 : 13-16. It is a beautiful allegory, which delights and instructs. It is a moral tale in which Oscar Widle has conveyed his strong religious feelings and deep understanding of the beautiful things in nature, "Whosoever shall not receive the kingdom of God as a little child he shall not enter there. The childlike innocence and belief make a man the true child of God. He makes a very ingenuons use of this Biblical story. His writing make an excellent use of paradox and epigram.

References

Spring, snow, Frost, Hail, Wind — they have been personified.

In one corner it was still winter — the child could not climb the tree an activity associated with summer.

For on the palm ... little feet — allusion to baby Christ and the marks on the palms refer to nailng of the palms on the cross.

Wounds of love — the concept of Christian God who loved the world & mankind that he sent his son, Christ, for their salvation. In Christ's teachings love is the most important factor.

❑

THE GIFT OF THE MAGI

O. HENRY

One dollar and eighty-seven cents. That was all.And sixty cents of it was in pennies. Pennies saved one and two at a time by bulldozing the grocer and the vegetable man and the butcher until ones' cheeks burned with the silent imputation of parsimony that such close dealing implied. Three times Della counted it. One dollar and eighty-seven cents. And the next day would be Christmas.

There was clearly nothing left to do but flop down on the shabby little couch and howl. So Della did it. Which instigates the moral reflection that life is made up of sobs, sniffles, and smiles, with sniffles predominating.

While the mistress ofthe home is gradually subsiding from the first stage to the second, take a look at the home. A furnished flat at $ 8 per week. It did not exactly beggar description, but it certainly had that word on the look-out for the mendicancy squad.

In the vestibule below was a letter-box into which no letter would go, and an electric button from which no mortal finger could coax a ring. Also appertaining thereunto was a card bearing the name 'Mr. James Dillingham Young.'

The 'Dillingham' had been flung to the breeze during a former period of prosperity when its possessor was being paid $ 30 per week. Now, when the income was shrunk to $ 20, the letter of 'Dillingham' looked blurred, as though they were thinking seriously of contracting to a modest and unassuming D. But whenever Mr. James Dillingham Young came home and reached his flat above he was called 'Jim' and greatly hugged by Mrs. James Dillingham Young, already introduced to you as Della. Which is all very good.

Dell finished her cry and attended to her cheeks with a powder rag. She stood by the window and looked out dully at a grey cat walking a grey fence in a grey backyard. To-morrow would be Christmas Day and she had only $ 1.87 with which to buy Jim a present. She had been saving every penny she could for months, with this result. Twenty dollars a week doesn't go far. Expenses had been greater than she had calculated. They always are. Only $1.87 to buy a present for Jim. Her Jim. Many a happy hour she had spent planning for something nice for him. Something fine and rare and sterling—something just a little bit near to being worthy of the honour of being owned by Jim.

There was a pier-glass between the windows of the room. Perhaps you have seen a pier-glass in an $ 8 flat. A very thin and very agile person may, by observing his reflection in a rapid sequence of longitudinal strips, obtain a fairly accurate conception of his looks. Della, being slender, had mastered the art.

Suddenly she whirled from the window and stood before the glass. Her eyes were shining brilliantly, but her face had lost its colour within twenty seconds. Rapidly she pulled down her hair and let it fall to its full length.

Now, there were two possessions of the James Dillingham Youngs in which they both took a mighty pride. One was Jim's gold watch that had been his father's and his grandfather's. The other was Della's hair. Had the Queen of Sheba lived in the flat across the airshaft, Della would have let her hair hang out of the window some day to dry just to depreciate Her Majesty's jewels and gifts. Had King Solomon been the Janitor, with all his treasures piled up in the basement, Jim would have pulled out his watch every time he passed, just to see him pluck at his beard from envy.

So now Della's beautiful hair fell about her, rippling and shining like a cascade of brown waters. It reached below her knee and made itself almost a garment for her. And then she did it up again nervously and quickly. Once she faltered for a minute and stood still while a tear or two splashed on the worn red carpet.

On went her old brown jacket; on went her old brown hat. With a whirl of skirts and with the brilliant sparkle still in her eyes, she fluttered out of the door and down the stairs to the street,

Where she stopped the sign read: 'Mme Sofronie. Hair Goods of All kinds.' One flight up Della ran, and collected herself, panting. Madame, large, too white, chilly, hardly looked the 'Sofronie.'

'Will you buy my hair?' asked Della.

'I buy hair,' said Madame. 'Take yer hat off and let's have a sight at the looks of it.'

Down rippled the brown cascade.

'Twenty dollars,' said Madame, lifting the mass with a practised hand.

'Give it to me quick,' said Della.

Oh, and the next two hours tripped by on rosy wings. Forget the hashed metaphor. She was ransacking the stores for Jim's present.

She found it at last. It surely had been made for Jim and no one else. There was no other like it in any of the stores, and she had turned all of them inside out. It was a platinum fob chain simple and chaste in design, properly proclaiming its value by substance alone and not by meretricious ornamentation—as all good things should do. It was even worthy of The Watch. As soon as she saw it she knew that it must be Jim's. It was like him. Quietness and value—the description applied to both. Twenty-one dollars they took from her for it, and she hurried home with the 87 cents. With that chain on his watch Jim might be proberly anxious about the time in any company. Grand as the watch was, he sometimes looked at it on the sly on account of the old leather strap that he used in place of a chain.

When Della reached home her intoxication gave way a little to prudence and reason. She got out her curling irons and lighted the gas and went to work repairing the ravages made by generosity added to love. Which is always a tremendous task, dear friends—a mammoth task.

Within forty minutes her head was covered with tiny,close-lying curls that made her look wonderfully like a truant schoolboy. She looked at her reflection in the mirror long, carefully, and critically.

'If Jim doesn't kill me,' she said to herself, 'before he takes a second look at me, he'll say I look like a Coney Island chorus girl. But what could I do—oh! what could I do with a dollar and eighty-seven cents?

At 7 o'clock the coffee was made and the frying-pan was on the back of the stove hot and ready to cook the chops.

Jim was never late. Della doubled the fob chain in her hand and sat on the corner of the table near the door that he always entered. Then she heard his step on the stair away down on the first flight, and she turned white for just a moment. She had a habit of saying little silent prayers about the simplest everyday things, and now she whispered: 'Please, God, make him think I am still pretty.'

The door opened and Jim stepped in and closed it. He looked thin and very serious. Poor fellow, he was only twenty-two—and to be burdened with a family! He needed a new overcoat and he was without gloves.

Jim stepped inside the door, as immovable as a setter at the scent of quail. His eyes were fixed upon Della, and there was an expression in them that she could not read, and it terrified her. It was not anger, nor surprise, nor disapproval, nor horror, nor any of the sentiments that she had been prepared for. He simply stared at her fixedly with that peculiar expression on his face.

Della wriggled off the table and went for him.

'Jim, darling,' she cried, 'don't look at me that way. I had my hair cut off and sold it because I couldn't have lived through Christmas without giving you a present. It'll grow out again—you won't mind, will you? I just had to do it. My hair grows awfully fast. Say "Merry Christmas!" Jim, and let's be happy. You don't know what a nice—what a beautiful nice gift I've got for you.'

'You've cut off your hair?' asked Jim, laboriously, as if he had not arrived at that patent fact yet, even after the hardest mental labour.

'Cut it off and sold it,' said Della. 'Don't you like me just as well, anyhow? I'm me without my hair, ain't I?'

Jim looked about the room curiously.

'You say your hair is gone?' he said, with an air almost of idiocy.

'You needn't look for it,' said Della. 'It's sold, I tell you—sold and gone, too. It's Christmas Eve, boy. Be good to me, for it went for you. May be the hairs of my head were numbered,' she went on with a sudden serious sweetness, 'but nobody could ever count mylove for you. Shall I put the chops on, Jim?'

Out of his trance Jim seemed quickly to wake. He enfolded his Della. For ten seconds let us regard with discreet scrutiny some unconsequential object in the other direction. Eight dollars a week or a million a year—what is the difference? A mathematician or a wit would give you the wrong answer. The magi brought valuable gifts, but that was not among them. This dark assertion will be illuminated later on.

Jim drew a package from his overcoat pocket and threw it upon the table.

'Don't make any mistake, Dell,' he said, 'about me. I don't think there's anything in the way of a haircut or a shave or a shampoo that could make me like my girl any less. But if you'll unwrap that package you may see why you had me going a while at first.'

White fingers and nimble tore at the string and paper. And then an ecstatic scream of joy; and then, Alas! a quick feminine change to hysterical tears and wails, necessitating the immediate employment of all the comforting powers of the lord of the flat.

For there lay The Combs—the set of combs, side and back, that Della had worshipped for long in a Broadway window. Beautiful combs, pure tortoise-shell, with jewelled rims—just the shade to wear in the beautiful vanished hair. They were expensive combs, she knew, and her heart had simply craved and yearned over them without the least hope of possession. And now, they were hers, but the tresses that should have adorned the coveted adornments were gone.

But she hugged them to her bosom, and at length she was able to look up with dim eyes and a smile and say: 'My hair grows so fast, Jim!'

And then Della leaped uplike a little singed cat and cried, 'Oh oh!'

Jim had not yet seen his beautiful present. She held it out to him eagerly upon her open palm. The dull precious metal seemed to flash with a reflection of her bright and ardent spirit.

'Isn't it a dandy, Jim? I hunted all over town to find it. You'll have to look at the time a hundred times a day now. Give me your watch. I want to see how it looks on it.'

Instead of obeying, Jim tumbled down on the couch and put his hands under the back of his head and smiled.

'Dell,' said he, 'let's put our Christmas presents away and keep' em a while. They're too nice to use just at present. I sold the watch to get the money to buy your combs. And now suppose you put the chops on.'

The magi, as you know, were wise men—wonderfully wise men—who brought gifts to the Babe in the manager. They invented the art of giving Christmas presents. Being wise, their gifts were no doubt wise ones, possibly bearing the privilege of exchange in case of duplication. And here I have lamely related to you the uneventful chronicle of two foolish children in a flat who most unwisely sacrificed for each other the greatest treasures of their house. But in a last word to the wise of these days let it be said that of all who give gifts these two were the wisest. Of all who give and receive gifts, such as they are wisest. Everywhere they are wisest. They are the magi.

THE GIFT OF THE MAGI

About the Author

O. Henry (William sydney porter) is a great American short story writer. His wonderful stories are marked by irony and wit. He democratized the language and used American slang. His imagination, humour and narrative skill give his stories a life of its own.

O. Henry is an accomplished American short story writer. This short story is certainly one of the best short stories even written. Jim and Della love each other and on the Christmas eve they wish to give a gift as the the magi had offered costly and traditional gifts to the newly born christ in the manger. But they have no money. So, Della sells off her beautiful hair to buy a gold wrist band for Jim's priceless gold watch. And Jim sells off his watch to buy tortoise shill comb for her beautiful hair. In their action governed by true love they give away the gold watch and beautiful cascade of hair — the prized possessions of the household. Love leads to willing sacrifice. The magi were wise men who give gifts to baby Christ but our magi 'Jim and Della are also wise in their own way. The irony is apparent.

His stories are immensely popular. He displays a rare skill to build up a climax and enthrall and surprise the readers with a dramatic ending. The unexpected turn at the end of the story is tremendously powerful and leaves deep emotional impact on the readers. His stories have been rendered on television serials and screens and have won warm response across the globe.

References

Imputation — attributed to fault
Parsimony — extreme economy
Whirled — to rotate or to turn around rapidly.
Queen of Sheba — she visited Soloman to test his legendary wisdom, beauty and wisdom
King Solomon — 10th B. C. King of Israel and son of David, an extra-ordinary wise man.
Unconsequential — without consequence or substance.

❑

MR KNOW ALL

MAUGHAM

I was prepared to dislike Max Kelada even before I knew him. The war had just finished and the passenger traffic in the ocean-going liners was heavy. Accommodation was very hard to get and you had to put up with whatever the agents chose to offer you. You could not hope for a cabin to yourself and I was thankful to be given one in which there were only two berths. But when I was told the name of my companion my heart sank. It suggested closed port-holes and the night air rigidly excluded. It was bad enough to share a cabin for fourteen days with anyone (I was going from San Francisco to Yokohama) but I should have looked upon it with less dismay if my fellow-passenger's name had been Smith or Brown.

When I went on board I found Mr. Kelada's luggage already below. I did not like the look of it; there were too many labels on the suitcases, and the wardrobe trunk was too big. He had unpacked his toilet things, and I observed that he was patron of the excellent Monsieur Coty; for I saw on the washing-stand his scent, his hair wash, and his brilliantine. Mr. Kelada's brushes, ebony with his monogram in gold, would have been all the better for a scrub. I did not at all like Mr. Kelada. I made my way into the smoking-room. I called for a pack of cards and began to play patience. I had scarcely started before a man came up to me and asked me if he was right in thinking my name was so-and-so.

'I am Mr. Kelada,' he added, with a smile that showed a row of flashing teeth, and sat down.

'Oh, yes, we're sharing a cabin, I think.'

'Bit of luck I call it. You never know who you're going to be put in with. I was jolly glad when I heard you were English. I'm all for us English sticking together when we're abroad, if you understand what I mean.'

I blinked.

'Are you English?' I asked, perhaps tactlessly.

'Rather. You don't think I look like an American, do you? British to the backbone, that's what I am.'

To prove it, Mr. Kelada took out of his pocket a passport and airily waved it under my nose.

King George has many strange subjects. Mr. Kelada was short and of a sturdy build, clean-shaven and dark-skinned, with a fleshy, hooked nose and very large, lustrous, and liquid eyes. His long black hair was sleek and curly. He spoke with a fluency in which there was nothing English, and his gestures were exuberant. I felt pretty sure that a closer inspection of that British passport would have betrayed the fact that Mr. Kelada was born under a bluer sky than is generally seen in England.

'What will you have?' he asked me.

I looked at him doubtfully. Prohibition was in force, and to all appearances the ship was bone-dry. When I am not thirsty I do not know which I dislike more, ginger-ale or lemon-squash. But Mr. Kelada flashed an oriental smile at me.

'Whisky and soda or a dry Martini, you have only to say the word.'

From each of his hip-pockets he fished a flask and laid them on the table before me. I chose the Martini, and calling the steward, he ordered a tumbler of ice and a couple of glasses.

'A very good cocktail,' I said.

'Well, there are plenty more where that came from, and if you've got any friends on board you tell them you've got a pal who's got all the liquor in the world.'

Mr. Kelada was chatty. He talked of New York and of San Frnacisco. He discussed plays, pictures, and politics. He was patriotic. The Union Jack is an impressive piece of drapery, but when it is flourished by a gentleman from Alexandria or Beirut I cannot but feel that it loses somewhat in dignity. Mr. Kelada was familiar. I do not wish to put on airs, but I cannot help feeling that it is seemly in a total stranger to put mister before my name when he addresses me. Mr. Kelada, doubtless to set me at my ease, used no such formality. I did not like Mr. Kelada. I had put aside the cards when he sat down, but now thinking that for this first occasion our conversation had lasted long enough, I went on with my game.

'The three on the four,' said Mr. Kelada.

There is nothing more exasperating when you are playing patience than to be told where to put the card you have turned up before you have had a chance to look for yourself.

'It's coming out, it's coming out,' he cried. 'The ten on the knave.'

With rage and hatred in my heart I finished. Then he seized the pack.

'Do you like card tricks?'

'No, I hate card tricks,' I answered.

'Well, I'll just show you this one.'

He showed me three. Then I said I would go down to the dining-room and get my seat at table.

'Oh, that's all right,' he said. 'I've already taken a seat for you. I thought that as we were in the same state-room we might just as well sit at the same table.'

I did not like Mr. Kelada.

I not only shared a cabin with him and ate three meals a day at the same table, but I could not walk round the deck without his joining me. It was impossible to snub him. It never occurred to him that he was not wanted. He was certain that you were as glad to see him as he was to see you. In your own house you might have kicked him downstairs and slammed the door in his face without the suspicion dawning on him that he was not a welcome visitor. He was a good mixer, and in three days he knew everyone on board. He ran everything. He managed the sweeps, conducted the auctions, collected money for prizes at the sports, got up quoit and golf matches, organized the concert, and arranged the fancy-dress ball. He was everywhere and always. He was certainly the best-hated man in the ship. We called him Mr. Know-All, even to his face. He took it as a compliment. But it was at meal times that he was most intolerable. For the better part of an hour then he had us at his mercy. He was hearty, jovial, loquacious, and argumentative. He knew everything better than anybody else, and it was an affront to his overweening vanity that you should disagree with him. He would not drop a subject, however unimportant, till he had brought you round to his way of thinking. The possibility that he could be mistaken never occurred to him. He was the chap who knew. We sat at the doctor's table. Mr. Kelada would certainly have had it all his own way, for the doctor was lazy and I was indifferent, except for a man called Ramsay, who sat there also. He was as dogmatic as Mr. Kelada and resented bitterly the Levantine,s cocksureness. The discussions they had were acrimonious and interminable.

Ramsay was in the American Consular Service, and was stationed at Kobe. He was a great heavy fellow from the Middle West, with loose fat under a tight skin, and he bulged out of his ready-made clothes. He was on his way back to resume his post, having been on a flying visit to New York to fetch his wife who had been spending a year at home. Mrs. Ramsay was a very pretty little thing, with pleasant manners and a sense of humour. The Consular Service is ill paid, and she was dressed always very simply, but she knew how to wear her clothes.

One evening at dinner the conversation by chance drifted to the subject of pearls. There had been in the papers a good deal of talk about the cultured pearls which the cunning Japanese were making, and the doctor remarked that they must inevitably diminish the value of real ones. They were very good already, they would soon be perfect. Mr. Kelada, as was his habit, rushed the new topic. He told us all that was to be known about pearls. I do not believe Ramsay knew anything about them at all, but he could not resist the opportunity to have a fling at the Levantine, and in five minutes we were in the middle of a heated argument. I had seen Mr. Kelada vehement as now. At last something that Ramsay said stung him, for he thumped the table and shouted:

'Well, I ought to know what I am talking about I'm going to Japan just to look into this Japanese pearl business. I'm in the trade, and there's not a man in it who won't tell you that what I say about pearls goes. I know all the best pearls in the world, and what I don't know about pearls isn't worth knowing.'

Here was news for us, for Mr. Kelada, with all his loquacity, had never told anyone what his business was. We only knew vaguely that he was going to Japan on some commercial errand. He looked round the table triumphantly.

'They'll never be able to get a cultured pearl that an expert like me can't tell with half an eye.' He pointed to a chain that Mrs. Ramsay wore. 'You take my word for it, Mrs.Ramsay, that chain you're wearing will never be worth a cent less than it is now.'

Mrs. Ramsay modestly flushed a little and slipped the chain inside her dress. Ramsay leaned forward. He gave us all a look, and a smile flickered in his eyes.

'That's a pretty chain of Mrs. Ramsay's, isn't it?'

'I noticed it at once,' answered Mr. Kelada. 'Gee, I said to myself, those are pearls all right.'

'I didn't buy it myself, of course, I'd be interested to know how much you think it cost.'

'Oh, in the trade somewhere round fifteen thousand dollars. But if it was bought on Fifth Avenue I shouldn't be surprised to hear that anything up to thirty thousand was paid for it.'

Ramsay smiled grimly.

'You'll be surprised to hear that Mrs. Ramsay bought that string at a department store the day before we left New York for eighteen dollars.'

Mr. Kelada flushed.

'Rot. It's not only real, but it's as fine a string for its size as I've ever seen.'

'Will you bet on it? I'll bet you a hundred dollars it's imitation.'

'Done.'

'Oh, Elmer, you can't bet on a certainty,' said Mrs. Ramsay.

She had a little smile on her lips and her tone was gently deprecating.

'Can't I? If I get a chance of easy money like that I should be all sorts of a fool not to take it.'

'But how can it be proved?' she continued. 'It's only my word against Mr. Kelada's.

'Let me look at the chain, and if it's imitation I'll tell you quickly enough. I can afford to lose a hundred dollars,' said Mr. Kelada.

'Take it off, dear. Let the gentleman look at it as much as he wants.' Mrs. Ramsay hesitated a moment. She put her hands to the clasp.

'I can't undo it,' she said. 'Mr. Kelada will just have to take my word for it.'

I had a sudden suspicion that something unfortunate was about to occur, but I could think of nothing to say.

Ramsay jumped up.

'I'll undo it.'

He handed the chain to Mr. Kelada. The Levantine took a magnifying glass from his pocket and closely examined it. A smile of triumph spread over his smooth and swarthy face. He handed back the chain. He was about to speak. Suddenly he caught sight of Mrs. Ramsay's face. It was so white that she looked as though she were about to faint. She was staring at him with wide and terrified eyes. They held a desperate appeal; it was so clear that I wondered why her husband did not see it.

Mr. Kelada stopped with his mouth open. He flushed deeply. You could almost *see* the effort he was making over himself.

'I was mistaken,' he said. 'It's a very good imitation, but of course as soon as I looked through my glass I saw that it wasn't real. I think eighteen dollars is just about as much as the damned thing's worth.'

He took out his pocket-book and from it a hundred-dollar bill. He handed it to Ramsay without a word.

'Perhaps that'll teach you not to be so cocksure another time, my young friend,' said Ramsay as he took the note.

I noticed that Mrs. Kelada's hands were trembling.

The story spread over the ship as stories do, and he had to put up with a good deal of chaff that evening. It was a fine joke that Mr. Know-All had been caught out. But Mrs. Ramsay retired to her state-room with a headache.

Next morning I got up and began to shave. Mr. Kelada lay on his bed smoking a cigarette. Suddenly there was a small scraping sound, and I saw a letter pushed under the door. I opened the door and looked out. There was nobody there. I picked up the letter and saw that it was addressed to Max Kelada. The name was written in block letters. I handed it to him.

'Who's this form?' He opened it. 'Oh!'

He took out of the envelope, not a letter, but a hundred-dollar bill. He looked at me, and again he reddened. He tore the envelope into little bits and gave them to me.

'Do you mind just throwing them out of the porthole?'

I did as he asked, and then I looked at him with a smile.

'No one likes being made to look a perfect damned fool,' he said.

'Were the pearls, real?'

'If I had a pretty little wife I shouldn't let her spend a year in New York while I stayed at Kobe,' said he.

At that moment I did not entirely dislike Mr. Kelada. He reached out for his pocket-book and carefully put in it the hundred-dollar note.

MR KNOW ALL

About the Author

Somerset Maugham (1874-1965) is a 20th century English novelist who was born in Paris. He is a widely travelled specially in the Far East. He shows a keeness of observation of life and human nature. The variety of human content and a dry, shrewd mastery of English language are special features of his writings.

This an interesting story is which Maugham throws light on the hidden recesses of human nature. The obvious vulgarity of Mr Kelada is nicely balanced by the surprising end of the story. The pearls were seen as real pearls by Mr. Kelada but Mr. Ramsay admits that they are imitation pearls. The expectation aroused in the mind is demolished by the revelation. This is a characteristic of a story in the Classical form. Mr. Know all, afterall doesn't know much.

References

Liners	— ocean-going passenger ships.
Agents	— travel agents who book accommodation on ships, trains and airoplanes.
San Fransisco to Yokohama	— from U.S.A. to Japan across the Pacific ocean.
Monsier Coty	— famous French manufacturer of cosmetics under the brand name of Coty. (Monsier means Mr.)
Patience	— a game of cards
Tactlessly	— bluntly with no consideration.
Hooked	— curved.
Prohibition	— legal ban specially on intoxcating drinks and now on smoking.
Snub	— response, contempt, ignoring
Mixer	— one with an open personality who mixes with people quickly.
Loquacious	— talkative, garrulous
Affront	— insult
Overweening	— excessive, egoistic.
Levantine	— inhabitant of East Mediteranian coast
Drop	— finish talking about.

❑

THE GOLDEN DEER

FROM THE RAMAYANA

While Rama and his companions rejoiced, one of the giants escaped to Lanka, the great city where he sought out Ravan, his king, seated upon a golden deer.

"King," he said, innumerable demons led by Khara have fallen on the field of battle with Rama. By some chance, I have been enabled to reach this place alive."

The king's eyes grew red with anger as he listened in disbelief to the tale of a young hermit slaying an army of giants.

"Who," he cried, "seeking his own death, has dared to kill my people? None in the world will be able to protect him, not even Indra, Yama or Vishnu himself. No man can save him who has defined me! I am the Lord of Time, the Consumer of Fire, the Death of Death itself!"

"There may be a way of destroying this hermit prince," said the warrior, "supremely virtuous and brave, none in the world is able to subdue him in his wrath. By means of his shafts, he is able to stop a river in its course and shatter the very sky with its stars and pianets! O Ten-necked One, Rama is wedded to one more beautiful than any woman on earth. In the full bloom of youth, and possessed of well-proportioned limbs, she is a jewel adorned by jewels. In loveliness, she surpasses all heavenly beings, dwellers of the stars and nagas. And Rama so loves her that if she were taken from him, his grief would be more than he could endure."

"Be it so!" roared the mighty Ravan. "Tomorrow, I shall, with a glad heart, bring back this fair woman and avenge the death of Khara and his men !"

But Taraka's son, Maricha, argued that Rama, that sleeping lion who hunted the giants as deer, should not be roused. "Do not hurl youself into that dreadful and bottomless ocean called Rama," he said, "whose bow is the crocodile, whose shafts are the rising waves, and whose battlefield is its waters. O king, return in peace to your capital and do not bring destruction to your land and subjects."

Just then his sister Surpanakha entered. There she saw Ravan shining in glory, surrounded by his ministers. Blazing like a flame, he resembled a great fire kindled on an altar. Unconquered by gods, gandharvas and rishis, he resembled death itself with wide-open jaws, his great chest and shoulders bare, exposing the battle scars from sword and spear and arrow as well as the marks ofAiravata's tusks. Holding high before the king her disfigured face, the princess told her tale oflove beside the flowing river, of jealousy beside the leafy bower, and of death and terror in the clearing near the brother's hermitage.

Her words caused Ravan's hair to stand on end Dismissing his ministers, he fixed in his resolve, went secretly to that part ofhis palace where his chariots were held in readiness. He commanded his driver to bring out his car.

Mounted on that golden chariot set with gems, the wheels of which made a sound like thunder, Ravan visited Maricha once again.

"I have resolved," he said, "to carry off Sita by force, and I now seek your help in this undertaking. Learn from me how you can best assist me! Assuming the form of a golden deer, flecked with silver, let yourself be seen near Rama's hermitage in the presence of Sita. Seeing that lovely doe, assuredly Sita will say to her lord and Lakshman, 'Do you capture it!'

"When they are far away and, by good fortune, Sita is left alone, I shall bear her away without hindrance."

"O great King, listen to my appeal !" Maricha pleaded. "Those who have recourse to flattery are easy to find but rare are those who are willing to listen to that speech which is severe yet salutary. An unprincipled monarch, such as you, is the slave of his passions which bring ruin on him, his people and his country."

But Ravan scorned his words of warning.

Maricha sighed and said : "If this must be, then let it be now. Come, we will go!"

Coming to the clearing near the hermitage Maricha changed himself into a ravishing deer, wonderful to behold, the points of his horns studded with gems, his skin dappled his mouth like a red lotus, his hoofs like emerald, his legs slender and well-proportioned. The whole forest and Rama's beautiful retreat were filled with the radiance of that form gleaming with all the colours of the rainbow.

In order to capture Sita's glances, the golden deer strayed here and there in the grass among the flowers, coming and going at will, sometime disappearing into the distance, then drawing neat again, gambolling playfully, until he was certain Sita had glimpsed the gold and silver of his skin.

"Come! Come quickly! O, qukckly come my lord! And you, Lakshman, hasten too!" Sita softly urged her husband and his brother. "I see a deer the like of which has never been looked upon be human eyes. How fair he is, and gentle! O, if only you could catch this wondrous creature, that we might keep him us as companion!"

The brothers turned their eyes in that direction and saw across the clearing the golden dappled deer.

"This brilliant creature, whose radiance rivals the sun," said Lakshaman thougtfully, "Is the wicked art of magic. Stay, do not seek to follow him. It is an illusion, born of cunning!"

As Lakshman was speaking thus, Sita, wholly captivated by this phantom, turned away from him and begged her husband : "Take him captive, O Great Warrior, he will serve as a plaything. His loveliness has charmed my heart! If you can capture this deer alive, his skin will be most precious, O Lion among Men, I shall delight to sit on his golden hide, strewn with *Kusha Grass*."

The graceful creature with his golden skin, his horns set with precious gems, shining like the rising sun, captivated Rama himself. He yielded to Sita's wish and made ready to capture the creature alive. Before he left, he asked his worried brother to guard the hermitage against any unsuspected danger nor leave it for a moment until he returned from the hunt.

Bearing his bow in his hand, Rama ran in the direction of the matchless deer and saw his golden prey in all his beauty, close to him. Fixing his eyes on the woodland creature as he fled into the forest, he saw him sometimes taking a single leap, and then, in order to lure him on, allowing him to draw closer Timid and fearful, the deer would leap into the air, at times in full view, and then disappear into the depth of the forest.

Rama finally stopped to rest in a shadow, ready to give up the fruitless chase. Suddenly, in a clearing within his arrow's reach, he saw the golden deer move slowly, feeding on the grass. He raised his bow and drew out a death-dealing arrow more brilliant than the sun's rays. Placing it firmly on his bow, he let fly that arrow which resembled a fiery serpent. It pierced the heart of the deer; and the quivering creature fell, mortally wounded.

"O Sita! O Lakshman!" the demon called out And his voice sounded like Rama's own.

Sita heard this frantic, piercing call for help. But Lakshman did not stir. "I promised Rama not to leave you," he reminded her.

"You do not love him! Else your feet would hasten you to your brother's side," cried Sita.

"Fear not for him, O most fair one!" Lakshman tried to calm her. "I vowed that I would safeguard you and not leave you until his return from the hunt."

At these words, Sita, her eyes flashing with anger, spoke in scorn : "What treachery is this? Can it be your hope that Rama's widow will become your bride? If anything should happen to my lord, I shall cast myself into the river! O base heart! O disgrace of the Kosalas!"

A heavy stillness seemed to fill the air when Sita was left alone. There was a deep silence all about her. Yet in her heart there was no peace. She blamed herself for the cruel words she had spoken to Lakshman; and she blamed herself even more for sending Rama in pursuit of the golden deer.

THE GOLDEN DEER

About the Author

The source of the Story—The story Golden Deer has been taken from Valmiki's Sanskrit **Ramayana**, a romantic epic depicting the life and deeds of Lord Rama, an incarnation of Vishnu. The style and language of **The Ramayan** are less rugged than those of **The Mahabharata**. The central scene of the epic is of course, Ayodhya, the capital of the old kingdom of Koshala. Other incidents of importance do take place sometimes in the midst of dense forest of Lanka, supposedly the kingdom of the demon king Ravana. The scene of the present story is the dense forest where Rama along with his younger brother Lakshman and Sita lived in banishment. It is the story of the days of exile of Rama.

❑

THE POSTMASTER

RABINDRANATH TAGORE

The Postmaster first took up his duties in the village of Ulapur. Though the village was a small one, there was an indigo factory near by, and the proprietor, and Englishman, had managed to get a post office established.

Our postmaster belonged to Calcutta. He felt like a fish out of water in this remote village. His office and living room were in a dark thatched shed, not far from a green, slimy pond, surrounded on all sides by a dense growth.

The men employed in the indigo factory had no leisure; moreover, they were hardly desirable companions for decent folk. Nor is a Calcutta boy an adept in the art of associating with others. Among strangers he appears either proud or ill at ease. At any rate, the postmaster had but little company; nor had he much to do.

At times he tried his hand at writing a verse or two. That the movement of the leaves and the clouds of the sky were enough to fill life with joy—such were the sentiments to which he sought to give expression. But God knows that the poor fellow would have felt it as the gift of a new life, if some genie of the Arabian Nights had in one night swept away the trees, leave and all, and replaced them with a macadamised road, hiding the clouds from view with rows of tall houses.

The postmaster's salary was small. He had to cook his own meals, which he used to share with Ratan, an orphan girl of the village, who did odd jobs for him.

When in the evening the smoke began to curl up from the village cow-sheds, and the cicalas chirped in every bush; when the faquirs of the Baul sect sang their shrill songs in their daily meeting-place, when any poet, who had attempted to watch the movement of the leaves in the dense bamboo thickets, would have felt a ghostly shiver run down his back, the postmaster would light his little lamp, and call out "Ratan."

Ratan would sit outside waiting for this call, and, instead of coming in at once, would reply: "Did you call me, sir?"

"What are you doing?" the postmaster would ask.

"I must be going to light the kitchen fire," would be the answer.

And the postmaster would say : "Oh, let the kitchen fire be for awhile; light me my pipe first."

At last Ratan would enter, with puffed-out cheeks, vigorously blowing into a flame a live coal to light the tobacco. This would give the postmaster an opportunity of conversing. "Well, Ratan," perhaps he would begin, "do you remember anything of your mother?" That was a fertile subject. Ratan partly remembered, and partly didn't. Her father had been fonder of her than her mother; him she recollected more vividly. He used to come home in the evening after his work, and one or two evenings stood out more clearly than others, like pictures in her memory. Ratan would squat on the floor near the postmaster's feet, as memories crowded in upon her. She called to mind a little brother that she had—and how on some bygone cloudy day she had played at fishing with him on the edge of the pond, with a twig for a make believe fishing-rod. Such little incidents would drive out greater events from her mind. Thus, as they talked, it would often get very late, and the postmaster would feel too lazy to do any cooking at all. Ratan would then hastily light the fire, and toast some unleavened bread, which, with the cold remnants of the morning meal, was enough for their supper.

On some evenings, seated at his desk in the corner of the big empty shed, the postmaster too would call up memories of his own home, of his mother and his sister, of those for whom in his exile his heart was sad, memories which were always haunting him, but which he could not talk about with the men of the factory, though he found himself naturally recalling them aloud in the presence of the simple little girl. And so it came about that the girl would allude to his people as mother, brother, and sister, as if she had known them all her life. In fact, she had a complete picture of each one of them painted in her little heart.

One noon, during a break in the rains, there was a cool soft breeze blowing; the smell of the damp grass and leaves in the hot sun felt like the warm breating of the tired earth on one's body. A persistent bird went on all the afternoon repeating the burden of its one complaint in Nature's audience chamber.

The postmaster had nothing to do. The shimmer of the freshly washed leaves, and the banked-up remnants of the retreating rain-clouds were sights to see; and the postmaster was watching them, and thinking to himself : "Oh, if only some kindered soul were near—just one loving human being whom I could hold near my heart": this was exactly, he went on to think, what that bird was trying to say, and it was the same feeling which the murmuring leaves were striving to express. But no one knows,or would believe, that such an idea might also take possession of an ill-paid village postmaster in the deep, silent midday interval of his work.

The postmaster sighed, and called out "Ratan". Ratan was then sprawling beneath the guava-tree busily engaged in eating unripe guavas. At the voice of her master, she ran up breathlessly, saying: "Were you calling me, Dada?" "I was thinking," said the postmaster, "of teaching you to read," and then for the rest of the afternoon he taught her the alphabet.

Thus, in a very short time, Ratan had got as far as the double consonants.

It seemed as though the showers of the season would never end. Canals, ditches, and hollows were all overflowing with water. Day and night the patter of rain was heard, and the croaking of frogs. The village roads became impassable, and marketing had to be done in punts.

One heavily clouded morning, the postmaster's little pupil had been long waiting outside the door for her call, but, not hearing it as usual, she took up her dog-eared book, and slowly entered the room. She found her master stretched out on his pallet, and, thinking he was resting, she was about to retire on tip-toe, when she suddenly heard her name—"Ratan!" She turned at once and asked: "Were you sleeping, Dada?" The postmaster in a plaintive voice said: "I am not well. Feel my head; is it very hot?"

In the loneliness of his exile, and in the gloom of the rains, his ailing body needed a little tender nursing. He longed to remember the touch on the forehead of soft hands with tinkling bracelets, to imagine the presence of loving womanhood, the nearness of mother and sister. And the exile was not disappointed. Ratan ceased to be a little girl. She at once stepped into the post of mother, called in the village doctor, gave the patient his pills at the proper intervals, sat up at night by his pillow, cooked his gruel for him, and every now and then asked: "Are you feeling a little better, Dada?"

It was some time before the postmaster, with weakened body, was able to leave his sick-bed. "No more of this," said he with decision. "I must get a transfer." He at once wrote off to Calcutta an application for a transfer, on the ground of the unhealthiness of the place.

Relieved from her duties as nurse, Ratan again took up her old place outside the door. But she no longer heard the same old call. She would sometimes peep inside furtively to find the postmaster sitting on his chair, or stretched on his pallet, and staring absent-mindedly into the air. While Ratan was awaiting her call, the postmaster was awaiting a reply to his application. The girl read her old lessons over and over again—her great fear was lest, when the call came, she might be found wanting in the double consonants. At last, after a week, the call did come one evening. With an overflowing heart Ratan rushed into the room with her— "Were you calling me, Dada?"

The postmaster said: "I am going away tomorrow, Ratan."

"Where are you going, Dada?"

"I am going home."

"When will you come back?"

"I am not coming back."

Ratan asked no other question. The postmaster, of his own accord, went on to tell her that his application for a transfer had been rejected, so he had resigned his post, and was going home.

For a long time neither of them spoke another word. The lamp went on dimly burning and from a leak in one corner of the thatch water dripped steadily into an earthen vessel on the floor beneath it.

After a while Ratan rose, and went off to the kitchen to prepare the meal; but she was not so quick about it as on other days. Many new things to think of had entered her little brain. When the postmaster had finished his supper, the girl suddenly asked him: "Dada, will you take me to your home?"

The postmaster laughed. "What an idea!" said he; but he did not think it necessary to explain to the girl wherein lay the absurdity.

That whole night, in her waking and in her dreams, the postmaster's laughing reply haunted her—"What an idea!"

On getting up in the morning, the postmaster found his bath ready. He had stuck to this Calcutta habit of bathing in water drawn and kept in pithers, instead of taking a plunge in the river as was the custom of the village. For some reason or other, the girl could not ask him about the time of his departure, so she had fetched the water from the river long before sunrise, that it should be ready as early as he might want it. After the bath came a call for Ratan. She entered noiselessly, and looked silently into her master's face for orders. The master said: "You need not be anxious about my going away, Ratan; I shall tell my successor to look after you." These words were kindly meant, no doubt: but inscrutable are the ways of a woman's heart!

Ratan had borne many a scolding from her master without complaint, but these kind words she could not bear. She burst out weeping, and said: "No, no, you need not tell anybody anything at all about me; I don't want to stay on here."

The postmaster was dumbfounded. He had never seen Ratan like this before.

The new incumbent duly arrived, and the postmaster, having given over charge, prepared to depart. Just before starting he called Ratan, and said: "Here is something for you; I hope it will keep you for some little time." He brought out from his pocket the whole of his month's salary, retaining only a trifle for his travelling expenses. Then Ratan fell at his feet and cried: "Oh, Dada, I pray you, don't give me anything, don't in any way trouble about me," and then she ran away out of sight.

The postmaster heaved a sigh, took up his carpet bag, put his umbrella over his shoulder, and, accompanied by a man carrying his many-coloured tin trunk, he slowly made for the boat.

When he got in and the boat was under way, and the rain-swollen river, like a stream of tears welling up from the earth, swirled and sobed at her bows, then he felt a sort of pain at heart; the grief-stricken face of a village girl seemed to represent for him the great unspoken pervading grief of Mother Earth herself. At one time he had an impulse to go back, and bring away along with him that lonesome waif, forsaken of the world. But the wind had just filled the sails, the boat had got well into the middle of the turbulent current, and already the village was left behind, and its outlying burning-ground came in sight.

So the traveller, borne on the breast of the swift-flowing river, consoled himself with philosophical reflections on the numberless meetings and partings going on in the world—on death, the great parting, from which none returns.

But Ratan had no philosophy. She was wandering about the post office in a flood of tears. It may be that she had still a lurking hope in some corner of her heart that her Dada would return, and that is why she could not tear herself away. Alas for the foolish human nature! Its fond mistakes are persistent. The dictates of reason take a long time to assert their sway. The surest proofs meanwhile are disbelieved. One clings desperately to some vain hope, till a day comes when it has sucked the heart dry and then it breaks through its bonds and departs. After that comes the misery of awakening, and then once again the longing to get back into the maze of the same mistakes.

THE POSTMASTER

About the Author

Rabindranath Tagore (1861-1941) was a remarkable personality and a siginificant contributor to the emerging history of Indian literature in English. Though he did not have a formal schooling and academic grind, he was keenly conscious of nature and life around him. By the time he was fifty, he became an eminent poet of Bengal with a distinction as a dramatist and prose writer. His poetry is devotional and mystical and all his writings show a rainbow richness of deep emotions and sentiments and a flamboyance of imagination.

The Postmaster is also a touching story of a Postmaster and his relationship with a little orphan girl who worked for him in the village, where he was posted. Her little mind with tender feelings for the postmaster whom she addresses as dada shows different shades of human reality.

References

Like a fish out of water — out of place, uncomfortable.

Kindred souls — near and dear

Meeting and partings — ways of life

Vain hope — false hope.

❑

THE COW OF THE BARRICADES

RAJA RAO

They called her Gauri for she came every Tuesday evening before sunset to stand and nibble at the hair of the Master. And the Master touched her and caressed her and he said: 'How are you, Gauri?' and Gauri simply bent her legs and drew back her tongue and, shaking her head, ambled round him and disappeared among the bushes. And till Tuesday next she was not to be seen. And the Master's disciples gathered grain and grass and rice-water to give her every Tuesday, but she refused it all and took only the handful of grain the Master gave. She munched it slowly and carefully as one articulates a string of holy words, and when she had finished eating, she knelt again, shook her head and disappeared. And the Master's disciples said: 'This is a strange creature, and they went to the Cotton Street and the Mango Street, and they went by the Ginning Mills and through the Weavers' Lines, but Gauri was nowhere to be seen. She was not even a god-dedicated cow, for never had a shop-keeper caught her eating the grams nor was she found huddled in a cattle-pound. People said, 'Only the Master could have such strange visitors, and they went to the Master and said: 'Master, can you tell us who this cow may be?' And the Master smiled with unquenchable love and fun and he said: 'She may be my baton-armed mother-in-law. Though she may be the mother of one of you. Perhaps she is the great Mother's vehicle.' And like to a mother, they put kunkum on her forehead and till Tuesday next they waited for Gauri.

But people heard of it here and people heard of it there, and they came with grain and hay and kunkum water saying, 'We have a strange visitor, let us honour her.' And merchants came saying, 'May be she's Lakshmi, the Goddess, and we may make more money next harvest,' and fell at her feet. And students came to touch her head and touch her tail, saying, 'Let me pass the examinations this year!' And young girls came to ask for husbands and widows to ask for purity, and the childless to ask for children. And so every Tuesday there was a veritable procession of people at the Master's hermitage. But Gauri would pass by them all like a holy wife among men, and going straight to the Master, would nibble at his hair and disappear among the bushes. People unable to take back the untouched offerings gave them to the river and the fishes jumped to eat them as at a festival; but the crocodile had disappeared from the whirls of the deep waters. And one fine morning the Master woke in his bed to hear the snake and the rat playing under him, for when the seeker finds harmony, the jackal and the deer and the rat and the serpent become friends. And Gauri was no doubt a fervent soul who had sought the paths of this world to be born a sage in the next, for she was so compassionate and true. There was only one other person whose hair she had nibbled—she had nibbled at the hair ofthe Mahatma. For the Mahatma loved all creatures, the speechful and mute.

Now at this time the Mahatma's men were fighting in the country against the red men's Government. The Mahatma said: 'Don't buy their cloth.' And people did not buy their cloth. The Mahatma said: 'Don't serve under them.' And people did not serve under them. And the Mahatma said: 'Don't pay their taxes.' And people did not pay the taxes. And people gathered, and bonfires were lit and processions were formed, and there were many men wounded and killed and many taken to prisons, but people would not pay taxes nor would they wear foregin clothes. And soldiers came from the cities, big men, and bearded men, with large rifles, and they said to some, 'You shall not leave the house after sunset'; and to some, 'You shall not ride a bicycle'; and to yet others, 'You shall not go out of the district.' And children carried blue cards when they were good, blue and red when they were a little wicked, and red when they were very wicked. And women could not go to the temples and marriages, and men could not go to the riverside to ease themselves in the morning. Life became intolerable and people moaned and groaned; but the red man's Government would rule the country, happen what may, and make men pay more and more taxes.

Then the men in the mills and factories said, 'We are with you, brothers', and the women said, 'We are with you, sisters', and the whole town became a battle-ground. For, when the soldiers had passed through the streets, the workers of the mills builded barricade after barricade. With stones and bamboos and bedsteads and carts and mill-stones and granary-baskets they build barricades, and the soldiers could not pass again. The Master came and said: 'No barricades in the name of the Mahatma, for much blood will be spilt,' but the workmen said, 'It is not with, "I love you, I love you," you can change the grinding heart of this Government.' And they built more and more barricades and put themselves behind these, and one day they were the masters of the town.

But the red man's Government was not fool's government. It sent for men from Peshawar and Pindi, while heavy cars were stationed at the Çity Gates, with guns to the left and guns to the right, and soldiers stood beside them, for the town would be taken, and cost what it might the red man's Government would govern.

And, though Gauri had neither the blue card nor the red card she now came every evening to the Master; she looked very sad, and somebody had even seen a tear, clear as a drop of the Ganges, run down her cheeks, for she was of compassion infinite and true.

And people were much affrighted, and they took the women and the children to the fields beyond and they cooked food beneath the trees and lived there—for the army of the Government was going to take the town and no woman or child would be spared. And doors were closed and clothes and vessels and jewels were hidden away, and only the workmen and the men ruled the city, and the Master was the head of them all, and they called him President. Patrols of young men in khadi and Gandhicap would go through the streets, and when they saw the old or the miserly peeping from behind the doors they called them and talked to them and led them to the camp by the fields, for the Master said there was danger and nobody could stay but the strong and the young. Grass grew beneath the eaves and dust of monsoon swept along the streets while the red men's trains brought armies after arimes, and everybody could see them for the station was down below and the town upon a hill. Barricades lay on the streets like corpse-heaps after the last plague, but the biggest of them all was in the Suryanarayana Street. It was as big as a chariot.

Men were hid behind it and waited for the battle. But the Master said, 'No, there shall be no battle, brothers.' But the workmen said again, 'It is not with, "I love you, I love you,' that you can change the grinding heart of this Government,' and they brought picks and scythes and crowbars, and a few Mohammedans brought their swords and one or two stole riffles from the mansions, and there was a regular fighting army ready to fall on the red man's men. And the Master went and said this and the Master went and said that, but the workmen said, 'We'll fight', and fight they would. So deep in despair the Master said, 'I resign from the Presidentship,' and he went and sat in meditationand rose into the worlds from which come light and love, in order that the city might be saved from bloodshed. And when people heard this they were greatly angered against the workmen, but they, the workmen were right and the Master was right, and they did not know which way the eye should turn. Owls hovered about even in midday light, and when dusk fell, all the stars hung so low that people knew that night would see the fight.

But everybody looked at the empty street-corners and said, 'Where is she—Gauri?'

At ten that night the first war-chariots were heard to move up, and cannons and bayonets and lifted swords rushed in assault.

And what happened afterwards people remember to this very day. There she was, Gauri, striding out of the Oil Lane and turning round Copper Seenayya's house towards the Suryanarayana Street, her head held gently bent and her ears pressed back like plaits of hair and staggering like one going to the temple with fruits and flowers to offer to the Goddess. And she walked fast, fast, and when people saw her they ran behind her, and crowds after crowds gathered round her and torch and lantern in hand they marched through the Brahmin Street and the Cotton Street and past the Venkatalakshamma well, and the nearer she came to the barricades the faster she walked, though she never ran. And people said, 'She will protect us. Now it's sure she will save us,' and bells were brought and rung and camphors were lit and coconuts were broken at her feet, but she neither shuddered nor did she move her head; she walked on. And the workmen who were behind the barricades, they saw this and they were more furious with it, and they said, 'Here, they send the cow instead of coming to help us.' Some swore and other laughed, and one of them said, 'We'll fire at her, for if the crowd is here and the red man's army on the other side it will be terrible.' But they were afraid, for the crowd chanted 'Vande Mataram', and they were all uplifted and sure, and Gauri marched onwards her eyes raised towards the barricades. And as she came near the Temple-square the workmen laid down their arms, as she came by the Tulsi Well they folded their hands, and as she was beneath the barricades they fell prostrate at her feet murmuring, 'Goddess, who may you be?' and they formed two rings, and between them passed Gauri, her left foreleg first, then her back right leg, once on the sand-bag, once on the cart-wheel, and with the third move men pushed her up and she was on the top of the barricades. And then came a rich whispering like a crowd at evening worship, but the red men's army cried from the other side of the barricades, 'Oh, what's this? Oh, what's this?' and they rushed towards the barricades thinking it was a flag of truce. But when they saw the cow and its looks and the tear, clear as a drop of the Ganges, they shouted out, 'Victory to the Mahatma! Mahatma Gandhi ki jai!' and joined up with the crowd. But their chief, the red man, saw this and fired a shot. It went through Gauri's head, and she fell a vehicle of God among lowly men.

But they said blood did not gush out of the head but only between the forelegs, from the thickness of her breast.

Peace has come back to us now. Seth Jamnalal Dwarak Chand bought the two houses on either side of the barricades, cut a loop road through them, and in the middle he erected a metal statue for Gauri. Our Gauri was not so tall nor was she so stiff, for she had a very human look. But we all offer her flowers and honey and perfumed sweetmeats and the first green grass of spring. And our children jump over the railings and play between her legs, and putting their mouths to the hole in the breast—for this was made too—shout out resounding booms. And never have our carpenters had gayer times than since Gauri died, for our children do not want their baswannabulls but only ask for Gauris. And to this day hawkers cry them about at the railway station, chanting, Gauris of Gorakhpur! Polished, varnished and on four wheels! and many a child from the far Himalayas to the seas of the South pulls them through the dusty streets of Hindusthan.

But even now when we light our sanctum lights at night, we say, 'Where is she, Gauri?' Only the Master knows where she is. He says : 'Gauri is waiting in the Middle Heavens to be born. She will be reborn when India sorrows again before She is free.'

Therefore it is said, 'The Mahatma may be all wrong about politics, but he is right about the fulness oflove in all creatures—the speechful and the mute.'

THE COW OF THE BARRICADES

About the Author

Raja Rao born in 1909 is an established novelist of Indian writing in English. He had his higher education at Hyderabad and Paris.He is a versatile genius with a keen mind which is at times intricate. His writings show a a strong awareness of Indian life which also form the content of his works. He is equally confident when he moves in the area of spiritualism. And it is this intertwining of mundane with spirituality which makes his works unique, difficult at times but always pleasant and alluring. **Kanthapura and The Serpent and the Rope** are two of his famous novels.

This excellent story presents a picture of Indian revolution which was made glorious by the leadership of an unknown Mahatma. The Indian involvement with Mahatmas who are embodiment of love and compassion has made this story a beautiful one. It reminds one of Gorky's mother, selfless commitment to other's welfare. Where is Gauri? is a question which reminds one of the famous Biblical question in Genesis, 'Where is your brother'? Rao in the story writes, 'Only the master knows.' This faith in the Divine is strongly presented though with a pinch. The Mahatma may be wrong about politics but is right about the fulness of love for all creatures.

References

Nibble	— to bite delicately
Munch	— to chew or to eat noisily.
Gush out	— to flow out with a force.
Sanctum	— sacred inner most part of a temple where Gods are installed. 'garbhgriha'

❑

AN ASTROLOGER'S DAY

R. K. NARAYAN

Punctually at midday he opened his bag and spread out his professional equipment, which consisted of a dozen cowrie shells, a square piece of cloth with obscure mystic charts on it, a notebook, and a bundle of palmyra writing. His forehead was resplendent with sacred ash and vermilion, and his eyes sparkled with a sharp abnormal gleam which was really an outcome of a continual searching look for customers, but which his simple clients took to be a prophetic light and felt comforted. The power of his eyes was considerably enhanced by their position—placed as they were between the painted forehead and the dark whiskers which streamed down his cheeks : even a half-wit's eyes would sparkle in such a setting. To crown the effect he would put a saffron-coloured turban around his head. This colour scheme never failed. People were attracted to him as bees are attracted to cosmos or dahlia stalks. He sat under the boughts of a spreading tamarind tree which flanked a path running through the Town Hall Park. It was a remarkable place in many ways: a surging crowd was always moving up and down this narrow road morning till night. A variety of trades and occupations was represented all along its way: medicine sellers, sellers of stolen hardware and junk, magicians, and, above all, an auctioneer of cheap cloth, who created din all day to attract the whole town. Next to him in vociferousness came a vendor of fried groundnut, who gave his ware a fancy name each day, calling it 'Bombay Ice Cream' one day, and on the next 'Delhi Almond,' and on the third 'Raja's Delicacy,' and so on and so forth, and people flocked to him. A considerable protion of this crowd detailed before the astrologer too. The astrologer transacted his business by the light of a flare which crackled and smoked up above the groundnut heap nearby. Half the enchantment of the place was dut to the fact that it did not have benefit of municipal lighting. The place was lit up by shop lights. One or two had hissing gaslights, some had naked flares stuck on poles, some were lit up by old cycle lamps, and one or two, like the astrologer's managed without lights of their own. It was a bewildering crisscross of light rays and moving shadows. This suited the astrologer very well, for the simple reason that he had not in the least intended to be an astrologer when he began life; and he knew no more of what was going to happen to others than he knew what was going to happen to himself next minute. He was as much a stranger to the stars as were his innocent customers. Yet he said things which pleased and astonished everyone : that was more a matter of study, practice, and shrewd guesswork. All the same, it was as much an honest man's labour as any other, and he deserved the wages he carried home at the end of a day.

He had left his village without any previous thought or plan. If he had continued there he would have carried on the work of his forefathers—namely tilling the land, living, marrying, and ripening in his cornfield and ancestral home. But that was not to be. He had to leave home without telling anyone, and he could not rest till he left it behind a couple of hundred miles. To a villager it is a great deal, as if an ocean flowed between.

He had a working analysisof mankind's troubles: marriage, money, and the tangles of human ties. Long practice had sharpened his perception. Within five minutes he understood what was wrong. He charged three pies per question, never opened his mouth till the other had spoken for at least ten minutes, which provided him enought stuff for a dozen answers and advices. When he told the person before him, gazing at his palm, 'In many ways you are not getting the fullest results for your efforts,' nine out of ten were disposed to agree with him. Or he questioned: 'Is there any woman in your family, may be even a distant relative who is not well disposed towards you?' Or he gave an analysis of character: 'Most of your troubles are due to your nature. How can you be otherwise with Saturn where he is? You have an impetuous nature and a rough exterior.' This endeared him to their hearts immediately, for even the mildest of us loves to think that he has a forbidding exterior.

The nuts vendur blew out his flare and rose to go home.This was a signal for the astrologer to bundle up too, since it left him in darkness except for a little shaft of green light which strayed in from somewhere and touched the ground before him. He picked up his cowrie shells and paraphernalia and was putting them back into his bag when the green shaft of light was blotted out; he looked up and saw a man standing before him. He sensed a possible client and said, 'You look so careworn. It will do you good to sit down for a while and chat with me.' The other grumbled some reply vaguely. The astrologer pressed his invitaiton; whereupon. the other thrust his palm under his nose, saying: 'You call yourself an astrologer?' The astrologer felt challenged and said, titling the other's palm towards the green shaft of light: 'Yours is a nature . . .' 'Oh, stop that,' the other said. 'Tell me something worthwhile . . .'

Our friend felt piqued. 'I charge only three pies per question, and what you get ought to be good enough for your money . . . ' At this the other withdrew his arm, took out an anna, and flung it our to him, saying: 'I have some questions to ask. If I prove you are bluffing, you must return that anna to me with interest.'

'If you find my answers satisfactory, will you give me five rupees?'

'No.'

'Or will you give me eight annas?'

'All right, provided you give me twice as much if you are wrong,' said the stranger. This pact was accepted after a little further argument. The astrologer sent up a prayer to heaven as the other lit a cheroot. The astrologer caught a glimpse of his face by the matchlight. There was a pause as cars hooted on the road, *jutka* drivers swore at their horses, and the babble of the crowd agitated the semi-darkness of the park. The other sat down, sucking his cheroot, puffing out, sat there ruthlessly. The astrologer felt very uncomfortable. 'Here, take your anna back. I am not used to such challenges. It is late for me today . . .' He made preparations to bundle up. The other held his wrist and said: 'You can't get out of it now. You dragged me in while I was passing.' The astrologer shivered in his grip; and his voice shook and became faint. 'Leave me today. I will speak to you tomorrow,' The other thrust his palm in his face and said: 'Challenge is challenge. Go on.' The astrologer proceeded with his throat drying up : 'There is a woman . . .'

'Stop,' said the other, 'I don't want all that. Shall I succeed in my present search or not? Answer this and go. Otherwise I will not let you go till you disgorge all your coins.' The astrologer muttered a few incantations and replied: 'All right I will speak. But will you give me a rupee if what I say is convincing? Otherwise I will not open my mouth, and you may do what you like.' After a good deal of haggling the other agreed. The astrologer said: 'You were left for dead. Am I right?"

'Ah, tell me more.'

'A knife has passed through you once?' said the astrologer.

'Good fellow!' He bared his chest to show the scar. 'What else?'

'And then you were pushed into a well nearby in the field. You were left for dead.'

'I should have been dead if some passer-by had not chanced to peep into the well,' exclaimed the other, overwhelmed by enthusiasm.

'When shall I get at him?' he asked, clenching his first.

'In the next world,' answered the astrologer. 'He died four months ago in a far-off town. You will never see any more of him.' The other groaned on hearing it. The astrologer proceeded:

'Guru Nayak—'

'You know my name!' the other said, taken a back.

'As I know all other things. Guru Nayak, listen carefully to what I have to say. Your village is two days' journey due north of this town. Take the next train and be gone. I see once again great danger to your life if you go from home.' He took out a pinch of sacred ash and held it to him. 'Rub it on your forehead and go home. Never travel southward again, and you will live to be a hundred.'

'Why should I leave home again?' the other said reflectively. 'I was only going away now and then to look for him and to choke out his life if Imet him.' He shook his head regretfully. 'He has escaped my hands. I hope at least he died as he deserved.' 'Yes,' said the astrologer. 'He was crushed under a lorry.' The other looked gratified to hear it.

The place was deserted by the time the astrologer picked up his articles and put them into his bag. The green shaft was also gone, leaving the place in darkness and silence. The stranger had gone off into the night, after giving the astrologer a handful of coins.

It was nearly midnight when the astrologer reached home. His wife was waiting for him at the door and demanded and explanation. He flung the coins at her and said: 'Count them. One man gave all that.'

'Twelve and a half annas,' she said, counting. She was overjoyed. 'I can buy some jaggery and coconut tomorrow. The child has been asking for sweets for so many days now. I will prepare some nice stuff for her.'

'The swine has cheated me! He promised me a rupee,' said the astrologer. She looked up at him. 'You look worried. What is wrong?'

'Nothing.'

After dinner, sitting on the *pyol*, he told her: 'Do you know a great load is gone from me today? I thought I had the blood of a man on my hands all these years. That was the reason why I ran away from home, settled here, and married you. He is alive.'

She gasped. 'You tried to kill ?'

'Yes, in our village, when I was silly youngster. We drank, gambled, and quarrelled badly one day—why think of it now? 'Time to sleep,' he said, yawning, and stretched himself on the *pyol*.

AN ASTROLOGER'S DAY

About the Author

R.K. Narayan (born 1906) ranks with Raja Rao and Mulk Raj Anand among the best Indian novelists writing in English. His novels and short-stories usually set in the fictitious town of Malgudi, deal with the Indian way of life and the Indian character with great maturity and artistry. His important novels are **Swami and Friends, The Bachelor of Arts, The Dark Room, The Financial Expert, Waiting for the Mahatma** and **The Guide.**

References

Cowrieshells — shell of snails

Palmyra writing — writing on palm leaves.

Resplendent — bright

Vociferous — noisy.

Impestuous Nature — rash nature

Jutka — a horse-drawn cart.

Sacred — pious

Gleam — glitter, brightness.

Vermillion — red powder like substance (Śindur)

Vender — seller of small articles on the road side.

❑

SPARROWS

K. AHMAD ABBAS

The sun was setting behind the mango grove which fringed the western extremity of the village when Rahim Khan returned from the fields. Broad and strong despite his fifty old years, with the plough on his shoulders, and driving his two oxen, he walked through the main street of the village with a haughty and unfriendly air. As he approached the *chaupal* where a dozen or so peasants were collected for their evening smoke, the hilarious tones of gossip died down to cautious whispers. It was only when he had vanished round the corner and the heavy tread of his footsteps was heard no more than Kallu, passing the communal *hookah* to another, remarked, 'There goes the hard-hearted devil!' To which Nanha, the fat sweet-seller, added: 'He is getting worse and worse every day. Only yesterday he beat poor Ramoo's child for throwing a pebble at his oxen.' Ramnath, the officious zaildar, volunteered further details of Rahim Khan's recent cruclties. 'And the other day he very nearly killed my mare for straying into his field.' The zaildar, of course, thought it quite irrelevant to mention that the straying of his mare had been specially planned by his own mischievous sons. The old grey-haired patel was, as usual, the last to open his toothless mouth. And as usual, his words were prefaced by a pious invocation to the Almighty. 'Hari Ram! Hari Ram!' he muttered, 'I have never seen such a cruel man. He has compassion neither for the child nor for the helpless animal. No wonder his own sons have run away from home.'

The subject of their conversation, meanwhile, had reached his hut which, almost symbolically stood gaunt and aloof, at a distance from the neighbouring cluster of houses. Leaning the plough up against the low wall of his house, he proceeded to tie the oxen to a pair of big wooden stakes embedded in the ground just in front of the doorway.

'Bhai Rahim Khan!' an obsequions voice said behind him as he was about to enter the house.

'What is it?' he gruffly queried, turning round to address the old woman who had come out of the house nearest his own. As she hesitated to speak he fired a volley of questions : 'What is it ? I won't eat you. Why don't you speak, woman? Has your son been arrested again for revenue arrears or has your daughter-in-law delivered another baby?'

As he stopped for breath, the woman summoned up all her courage to utter two words, 'Your wife . . . ' . . . has run away.' He completed the sentence with a grin, which broadened with the realization that he had guessed right.

'No, no,' the woman hastily explained with an apologetic look, as if she herself were responsible for his wife's absence. 'She has only gone to her brother at Nurpur and will be back in a few days.'

'Bah!' he flung back at her, opening the door. He knew that his wife would never come back.

Seething with inward wrath he entered the dark hut and sat down on the charpoy. A cat mewed in a corner. Finding no one else on whom to vent his anger he flung it out, slamming the door with violence.

There was no one to give him water to wash his dust-laden feet and hands, no one to give him supper, no one whom he could curse and beat. Rahim Khan felt uncomfortable and unhappy. He had always been angry with his wife when she was there, but her absence angered him still more.

'So she's gone,' he mused, lying down on the cot, having decided to go to sleep without his food. During the thirty years of their married life he had always felt that she would leave him one day and, at one time, he had even hoped she would. Six years ago, his eldest son Bundu had run away from home because of a more than usually severe beating. Three years later, the younger one, Nuru, joined his brother. Since that day, Rahim Khan felt sure his wife too would run away to her brother's house. But now that she had gone, he felt unhappy—not sorry, no, for he had never loved his wife—but only uncomfortable, as if a necessary piece of furniture had been removed. With her gone, on whom could he shower the outpourings of an embittered heart?

For thirty years his wife had been both the symbol and target of all his grievances against family, against society, against life.

As a youth there had been none in the village to beat him in feats of athletic skill—in wrestling, in kabadi, in diving from the canal bridge. He had loved a girl, and had wanted to join a touring circus which happened to pass through the village. In the circus, he had felt, lay the key to his ambitions—a career after his own heart—travel—fame. And in Radha, the daughter of Ram Charan, the village banya, he thought he had found his soul-mate. He had first noticed her watching him at a wrestling match and it had been the greatest moment of his life when, standing up after vanquishing his adversary, he had found Radha looking at him with the light of love in her eyes. After that there had been a few brief and furtive meetings when the unlettered but romantic youth had declared his love in passionate though halting words. But his parents had killed both ambitions. Circus work was too lowly and immoral for a respectable peasant. Anyway, his father, grandfather and all his ancestors had tilled the land, so he too had to do it. As for marrying Radha, a Hindu, a Kafir, the very idea was infamous and irreligious.

For some time, Rahim Khan, with youthful resentment, toyed with the idea of open rebellion. But the tradition of centuries of serfdom ran in his blood and, however, indignant he might have felt at his father's severity, he could not summon enough courage to defy paternal authority and social traditions. After a few days, the circus left the village without Rahim Khan, and the furtive romance with Radha, too, came to an abrupt end. Rahim Khan's father slyly suggested to Ram Charan that his daughter was now fifteen and ought to have been married long ago, not failing to hint at the disastrous consequences of late marriages. Within a few weeks Radha was married to Ram Lal, a middle-aged, pot-bellied banya of the neighbouring village. With a few sad tears shed in the solitude of the night in memory of her hopeless romance with Rahim Khan, she quickly reconciled herself to her fate and proceeded forthwith to be the mother of half-a-dozen children.

Rahim Khan also married. He had, of course, no choice in the matter. His parents selected the girl, fixed the date, ordered some gaudy clothes for him and some silver ornaments for his bride, sat him on a horse and, to the beat of a brass band, took him to the girl's house where the Nikah was duly performed. To the Kazi's formal questions Rahim Khan mechanically nodded his head. Any other course was impossible. Nobody, of course, cared to ask the shy little girl who sat huddled in a dark room only dimly conscious of the fate to which she had been condemned. After the ceremony, Rahim Khan's father, in a mood of self-congratulation, boasted to his wife : 'See how meekly he obeyed me. You always feared he might refuse to fall in with our arrangements. I know these youngsters. They are apt to be restless if their marriage is delayed. That is why our fathers believed in marrying away their children early. Now he will be all right!'

At that very moment, standing on the threshold of the room where his wife awaited him much as a sheep awaits the butcher, Rahim Khan made a terrible resolve to avenge himself on his parents, his family, on society. He held them all responsible for the frustration of his life's dreams. And in his confused, illogical mind he regarded his bride as the symbol of the persecution to which he had been subjected. On her he would wreak his vengeance. Iron entered his hitherto kindly soul as he rudely pushed open the door.

That was thirty years ago, Rahim Khan reflected as he lay there on his cot in the dark hut. And hadn't he had his revenge? For thirty years he had illtreated his wife, his children and his bullocks, quarrelled with everyone in the village and made himself the most hated person in the whole community. The thought of being so universally detested gave him grim satisfaction.

No one in the village, of course, understood or tried to understand the reasons for this strange transformation ofthe cheerful and kind young man into the beast that he had become. At first, their attitude towards him was one of astonished hostility, but later it changed to indifference mingled with fear. Of understanding and sympathy he received none. Shunned by everyone, with a bitterness ever gnawing at his heart, Rahim Khan sought consolation in the unquestioned authority over his wife which society allowed him.

For thirty years his wife had submitted to his persecution with the slave-like docility that is the badge of her tribe. Lately, indeed, she had become so used to corporal chastisement that it seemed unnatural if a whole week passed without a beating. To Rahim Khan beating his wife had become a part of his very existence. As sleep gathered round him, his last thought was whether he would be able to endure a life without having an opportunity of indulging in what had now become his second nature. It was perhaps the only moment when Rahim Khan had a feeling, not exactly of affection, for his wife, but of loneliness without her. Never before had he realized how much the woman he hated was a part of his life.

When he awoke it was already late forenoon and he started the day by cursing his wife, for it was she who used to wake him early every morning. But he was in no great hurry today. Lazily he got up and, after his ablutions, milked the goats for his breakfast which consisted of the remains of the previous day's chapattis soaked in the fresh milk. Then he sat down for a smoke, with his beloved *hookah* beside him. Now the hut was warm and alight with the rays of the sun streaming in through the open window. In a corner they revealed some cobwebs and, having already decided to absent himself from his fields, he thought he would tidy his hut. Tying some rags to the end of the long pole, he was about to remove the cobwebs when he saw a nest in the thatched roof. Two sparrows were fluttering in and out, twittering constantly.

His first impulse was to wreck the nest with one stroke of his pole, but something within him made him desist. Throwing down the pole, he brought a stool and climbed up on it to get a better view of the sparrows home. Two little featherless mites of red flesh, baby sparrows hardly a day old, lay inside, while their parents hovered round Rahim Khan's face, screaming threateningly. He barely had a glimpse of the inside of the nest when the mother sparrow attacked him.

'Oh damn, you vixen, you might have plucked out my eye,' exclaimed Rahim Khan with his characteristic hollow laugh, and climbed down from his perch. He was strangely amused by the little bird's heroic efforts to save their home and children. The sparrows' nest suffered no harm that day and peace reigned in Rahim Khan's hut.

Next day he resumed his daily work. Still no one talked to him in the village. From morning till late in the afternoon he would toil in the field, ploughing the furrow and watering the crops, but he returned home before sunset. Then he would lie on his cot, smoking his *hookah* and watching with lively interest the antics of the sparrow family. The two little ones had now grown into fine young birds, and he called them Nuru and Bundu after his lost sons whom he had not seen for several years, The four sparrows were his only friends in the world. His neighbours were still frightened of him and regarded his recent peaceful behaviour with suspicion. They were genuinely astonished that for some time no one had seen him beating his bullocks. Nathoo and Chhiddo themselves were happy and grateful and their bruised bodies had almost healed.

One monsoon evening, when the sky was overcast with threatening clouds, Rahim Khan returned from the fields a little earlier than usual. He found a group of children playing on the road. They ran away as they saw him, and even left their shoes behind in their haste. In vain did Rahim Khan shout, 'Why are you running away? I am not going to beat you.' Meanwhile, it had started drizzling and he hurried homewards to tie up the bullocks before the big downpour came.

Entering his hut,Rahim Khan lighted the earthenware oil lamp and placed some crumbs of bread for the sparrows before he prepared his own dinner. 'O Nuru! O Bundu!' he shouted, but the sparrows did not come out. Anxious to find out what had happened to his friends, he peered into the nest and found the quartet scared and sitting huddled up within their feathers. At the very spot where the nest lay, the roof was leaking. Rahim

Khan took a ladder and went out in the pouring rain to repair the damage. By the time the job was satisfactorily done he was thoroughly drenched. As he sat on the cot, Rahim Khan sneezed, but he did not heed the warning and went to sleep. Next morning he awoke with a high fever.

When the villagers did not see him going to the fields for several days they grew anxious and some of them came to see what was the matter. Through a crack in the door they saw him lying on the cot talking, so they thought, to himself. 'O Bundu, O Nuru, who will feed you when I am gone?'

The peasants shook their heads sympathetically. 'Poor fellow,' they said, 'he has gone mad. We will send for his wife to look after him.'

Next morning when Rahim Khan's wife, anxious and weeping, came with her sons, a group of neighbours collected in sympathy. The door was locked from the inside, and in spite of loud knocking no one opened it. When they broke their way in they found the large and gaunt frame of Rahim lying in the brooding silence of the room, broken only by the flutterings of four sparrows.

SPARROWS

About the Author

K. A. Abbas (1914–1987) is a journalist, short-story writer, novelist and film director. His versatelity is amazing. His literary out-put however, is small. K.A. Abbas came into prominence as a journalist on the staff of **The Bombay Chronicle**. He initiated The people's theatre movement after finding the Indian theatre in artistic and primitive. A widely travelled man, he also wrote a book on travels called **Outside India**. In his book of short stories, **Rice and other stories** he has depicted with sympathy the life of often dispised and neglected people who live in misery, poverty and squalor in Indian village and town. His sense of righteousness is often outraged by what he sees. In his novel **Inquilab** he portrays the struggle of Indian masses against the British during the hectic days of Non-co-operation movement. In his recent book of stories, **One Thousand Nights on a Bed of Stone** he has given a picturesque description of independent India. Each story spotlights some important aspect of Indian Life in the wake of freedom including the terrible tragedy of the partition. In all his stories he is occupied with bringing out the human side of his characters, often painted in strong and vivid colour to impress. His sense of drama is great; and he makes effective use of dramatic situation. His latest book is a biography of late Prime Minister Indira Gandhi.

References

Fringed	— adorned as a fringe or border
Commual hookah	— a hookah shared by all.
Patel	— the headman of a village.
Obsequious	— servile
Charpoy	— a common bed.
Banya	— an Indian trader.
Fertive	— secret
Kafir	— an unbeliever,
Docility	— passive obedience.
The badge of her tribe	— the characteristic of the class of wives,
Second nature	— acquired habit.
Oblutions	— washing of the body or a part of it.
Vixen	— a female fox.

❑

THE FLOOD

KAMALA MARKANDAYA

Nature is like a wild animal that you have trained to work for you. So long as you are vigilant and walk warily with thought and care, so long will it give you its aid; but look away for an instant, be heedless or forgetful, and it has you by the throat.

My daughter Ira had been given in marriage in the month of June, and what with the preparing for it, and the listlessness that took hold of me in the first days after her departure, nothing was done to make our hut weatherproof or a to secure the land from flooding. That year the monsoon broke early with and evil intensity such as non could remember before.

It rained so hard, so long, and so incessantly that the thought of a period of no rain provoked a mile wonder. It was as if nothing had ever been but rain, and the water pitilessly found every hole in the thatched roof to come in, dripping on to the already damp floor. If we had not built on high ground the very walls would have melted in that moisture. I brought out as many pots and pans as I had, and we laid them about to catch the drips, but soon there were more leaks than we had vessels ..... Fortunately, I had laid in a stock of firewood for Ira's wedding, and the few sticks that remained served at least to cook our rise, and while the fire burnt, hissing at the water in the wood, we huddled round trying to get dry. At first the children were cheerful engouh—they had not known such things before, and the lakes and small streams that formed outside gave them endless delight; but Nathan and I watched with heavy hearts while the waters rose and rose and the tender green of the paddy field sank under and was lost.

'It is a bad season,' Nathan said sombrely. 'The rains have destroyed much of our work; there will be little eating done this year.'

At these words, Arjun broke into doleful sobs and his brother, Thambi, followed suit. They were old enough to understand, but the others, who weren't, burst into tears too, for by now they were cramped and out of humour with sitting crouched on the damp floor; and hungry since there was little to eat, for most of the food had gone to make the wedding feast, and the new season's harvesting lay outside ungathered and rotting. I hushed them as best as I could, throwing a reproachful glance at my husband for his careless words, but he was unnoticing, sunk in hatred and helplessness.

As night came on—the eighth night of the monsoon—the winds increased, whining and howling ground our hut as if seeking to pluck it from the earth. Indoors it was dark—the wick, burning in its shallow saucer of oil, threw only a dim, wavering light—but outside the land glimmered, sometimes pale and sometimes vivid, in the flicker of lighting. Towards midnight the storm was as its worst. Lightning kept clawing at they sky almost continuously, thunder shook the earth. I shivered as I looked—for I could not sleep, and even a prayer come with difficulty.

'It cannot last' Nathan said. 'The storm will go down by the morning.'

Even as he spoke, a streak of lighting threw itself down at the earth. There was a tremendous clap of thunder, and when I uncovered my shrinking eyes I asw that our coconut plant had been struck. That, too, the storm had claimed for its own.

In the morning everything was clam. Even the rain had stopped. After the fury of the night before, an unnatural stillness lay on the land. I went out to see if anything could be saved of the vegetables, but the shoots and vines were battered and broken, torn from their supports and bruised; they did not show much sign of surviving. The corn field was lost. Our paddy field lay beneath a placid lake on which the children were already sailing bits of wood.

Many of our neighbours fared much worse than we had. Several were homeless, and of a group of men who had sheltered under a tree when the storm began six had been killed by lightning.

Kali's hut had been completely destroyed in the last final fury of the storm. The roof had been blown away bodily, the mud walls had crumbled.

'At least it stood until the worst was over', said Kali to me, 'and by God's grace we were all spared.' She looked worn out; in the many years I had known her I had never seen her so deflated. She had come to ask for some palm leaves to thatch the new hut her husband was building; but I could only point to the blackened tree, its head bitten off and hanging by a few fibres from the withered stump.

'We must thatch our roof before the night,' I said. 'The rains may come again. We need rice too.'

Nathan nodded. 'We may be able to buy palm laves in the village—also rice."

He went to the granary, in a corner of which the small cloth bundle of our savings lay buried. It had been heavy once, when we were newly married : now the faded rag in which it tied was too big and the ends flapped loosely over the knot. Nathan united it and counted out twelve rupees.

'One will be enough,' I said. 'Let us go.'

'I will take two. We can always put it back.'

In the village the storm had left disaster and desolation worse than on our own doorstep. Uprooted trees sprawled their branches in ghastly fashion over streets and houses, flattening then and the bodies of men and women. Sticks and stones lay scattered wildly in angry conftion. The tannery stood, its bricks and cement had held it together in spite of the raging winds; but the worker's huts, of weaker construction, had been demolished. The thatch had been ripped from some; where others stood there was now only a heap of mud with their owners possessions stuck in them in a kind of pitiless decoration. The corrugated-iron shacks in which some of the men lived were no more; here and there were we could see the iron sheets in unexpected places—suspended from tree tops, or blown and driven into the walls of houses still left standing. There were water everywhere, the gutters were overflowing into the streets. Dead dogs, cats, and rats cluttered the road-side, or floated on the waters with blown, distended bellies.

People were moving about amid this destruction, picking out a rag here, a bundle there, hugging those things that they thought to be theirs, moving uncertainly and with a kind of despair about them. People we know came and spoke to us in low voices, gesturing hopelessly.

'Let us go, it is no good; we'll come back later.'

We turned back, the two rupees unspent. Our children came running out to meet us, their faces bright with hope.

'The shops are closed or destroyed,' I said, 'Go inside, I will get you some gruel presently.'

Their faces faded; the two younger ones began crying listlessly from hunger and disappointment. I had no words to comfort them.

At dusk the drums of calamity began; their grave, throbbing rhythm came clearly through the night, throughout the night, each beat, each tattoo, echoing the mighty impotence of our human endeavour. I listened. I could not sleep. In the sound of the drums I understood a vast pervading doom; but in the expectant silence between, my own disaster loomed large more important, and more hurtful.

We ventured out again when the waters had subsided a little, taking with us as before two rupees. This time things were somewhat better; the streets were clear, huts were going up everywere. My spirits rose.

'To Hanuman, first for rice,' said Nathan, excited. 'The gruel we have been swallowing has been almost plain water these last few days.'

I quickened my steps; my stomach began heaving at the thought of food.

Hanuman was standing in the doorway of his shop. He shook his head when he saw us. 'You have come for rice,' he said. 'They all come for rice. I have none to sell, only enough for my wife and children.'

'And yet you are a merchant who deals in rice ?'

'And what if so ? Are you not growers of it ? Why, then, do you come to me ? If I have rice, I do not choose to sell it now; but I have told you, I have none'.

'We ask for only a little. We will pay for what we have—see, here is the money.'

'No, no rice but—wait.....they say Biswas is selling.....you can try.....'

To Biswas. 'We come for rice. Look, here is our money.'

'Two rupees ? How much do you think you can buy with two rupees ?'

'We thought—'

'Never mind what you thought ! Is this not a time of scarcity ? Can you buy rice anywhere else ? Am I not entitled to charge more for that ?'

'It is very little for two ruppes—'

'Take it or leave it. I can get double that sum from the tanners, but because I know you—'

We take it, we give up the silver coins. Now there is nothing left for the thatching, unless we use a rupee or two from the ten that remain in the granary.

I put the rice in my sari, tuck the precious load securely in at the waist. We turn back. On the outskirts of the village there is Kenny. His face is grim and long, his eyes are burning in his pale face. He sees us and comes up.

'You, too, are starving, I suppose'.

I tap the roll at my waist—the grains give at my touch.

'We have a little rice—it will last us unitll times are better.'

'Times are better, times are better,' he shouts. 'Times will not be better for many months. Meanwhile you will suffer and die, you meek suffering fools. Why do you keep this ghastly silence ? Why do you not demand—cry out for help—do something ? There is nothing in this country, Oh God, there is nothing ?

We shrink from his violence. What can we do—what can he mean ? The man is mad. We go on our way.

The paddy was completely destroyed; there would be no rice until the next harvesting. Meanwhile, we lived on what remained of our salted fish, roots and leaves, the fruit of the prickly pear, and on the plantains from our tree. At last the time came for the rice terraces to be drained and not ready for the next sowing. Nathan told me of it with cheer in his voice, and I told the children, pleasurably, for the fields were full of fish that would feed us for many a day. Then we waited, spirits lifting, eyes sparkling, bellies painful with anticipation.

At last the day, Nathan went to break the dams and I with him and with me our children, sunken-eyed, noisy as they had not been for many days at the thought of the feast, carrying nets and baskets. First one hole, then another, no bigger than a finger's width, until the water eroded the sides and the outlets grew large enough for two fists to go through. Against them we held our nets, feet firm in the mud while the water rushed away, and the fish came tumbling into them. When the water was all gone there they were caught in the "meshes and among the paddy, shoals of them leaping madly, wet and silver and good to look upon. We gathered them with flying fingers and greedy hearts and bore them away in triumph, with a glow at least as bright as the sun on those shining scales. Then we came and gathered up what remained of the paddy and took it away to thresh and winnow.

Late that night we were sill at work, cleaning the fish, hulling the rice, separating the grain from the husk. When we had done, the rice yield was meagren no more than two measures—all that was left of the year's harvest and the year's labour.

We ate, finding it difficult to believe we did so. The good food lay rich, if uneasy, in our starved bellies. Already the children were looking better, and at the sight of their faces, still thin but content, a great weight lifted from me. Today we would eat and tomorrow, and for many weeks while the grain lasted. Then there was the fish, cleaned, dried, and salted away and before that was gone we should earn some more money; I would plant more vegetables ...... such dreams, delightful, orderly, satisfying, but only dreams. And sleep, such sleep ... deep and sweet and sound as I had not known for many nights; it claimed me even as sat amied the rice husks and fish sacles and drying salt.

THE FLOOD

About the Author

Kamla Markandaya is one of the contemporary Indian novelists writing in English. Married to an English journlist, she lives abroad but her Indian past forms a texture of her stance as a writer. She has written a good number of novels on the varied themes of poverty, exodus to urban areas, cultural dualism, growing sense of alienation and changing patterns of life in India. She has the advantage of having the experience of both cultures which imparts authenticity and subtle nuance of Indian social, historical and cultural life portrayed in her novels.

Kamla Markandaya in her very first novel **Nector in a Sieve** presents fears of peasants when new industries threatened their landscape and life. Where was the dream of nectar ? She wrote a number fo novels. Her prose has the richness of sufficiency and suggestiveness. In her later novels she has bought out the "quiet despeation" in which most of the city dwellers live comdemned to live a life of pettiness and horror, pity and heroism.

References

Heavy hearts — discouraged hearts
Distended — swollen
Doleful — sorrowful
Listlessly — timid & dull manner
Tattoo — signal on a dream. (It also means making of the skin by indelible patterns, picture etc.)
Coconut palm — in south India one's prosperity may be judged by the number of palm trees.
Placid — calm
Terraces — fields cut out of a hill or rising land, on several levels.
Anticipation — expectation
Eroded — to wash away
Meagre — small

❑